# The Mechanics of Miracles

*How God's Invisible Spirit Manifests Tangibly*

**Propiv Press**
**Lancaster Pennsylvania, USA**

# The Mechanics of Miracles

*How God's Invisible Spirit Manifests Tangibly*

**By Jonathan Brenneman**
Foreword by J.D. King

# The Mechanics of Miracles

Copyright ©2023 by Jonathan Brenneman. All rights reserved. This book is protected by the copyright laws of the United States of America. This book may not be copied or reprinted for commercial gain or profit. The use of short quotations or occasional page copying for personal or group study is permitted and encouraged. Permission will be granted upon request.

Propiv Press, Lancaster, Pennsylvania, USA
ISBN- 9798329117837

Unless otherwise indicated, scripture quotations are taken from the New Revised Standard Version Bible, copyright © 1989 the Division of Christian Education of the National Council of the Churches of Christ in the United States of America. Used by permission. All rights reserved.

Scripture quotations marked NIV are taken from THE HOLY BIBLE, NEW INTERNATIONAL VERSION®, NIV® Copyright © 1973, 1978, 1984, 2011 by Biblica, Inc.® Used by permission. All rights reserved worldwide. Scripture quotations marked NKJV are taken from the New King James Version®. Copyright © 1982 by Thomas Nelson. Used by permission. All rights reserved. Scripture questions marked AMPC are taken from the Amplified® Bible, Copyright © 1954, 1958, 1962, 1964, 1965, 1987 by The Lockman Foundation. Used by permission. lockman.org. Scripture quotations taken from Young's Literal Translation are in public domain.

# Acknowledgements

Many people's insights have helped form my thinking. Although this book doesn't specifically cite Bill Johnson, his writings played an important role in helping me begin to understand Jesus' incarnation. Many of Bill's critics do not fully accept the Biblical truth that Jesus came not only as 100% God, but also as 100% human.

Bill, Randy Clark, and Joe McIntyre spoke at the conference that ignited a life of miracles for me. A few years later, Dan Mohler's teaching and example helped me to grow in faith and begin praying for people outside of religious contexts.

Jeff Randle's insights about "heart art" and the workings of God's power resonated with my experience and helped me to grow in understanding the mechanics of miracles. His insights added to some things I already knew but didn't yet know how to articulate clearly.

I also want to thank my mom, my dad, and the many Facebook friends and blog readers who provided feedback and made suggestions as I was preparing to publish this book.

# What People Are Saying

*The Mechanics of Miracles* is powerful and transformative. Jonathan provides an extremely in-depth exploration of the principles of healing, backing every insight with multiple Bible scriptures and real-life examples.

This book removes excuses and arguments, making understanding God's will and the practical dynamics of healing very clear. Your faith and boldness will increase with ease as you engage with and act on this guide to achieving healing results.

Fielding GoHarvest – Missionary & Healing Evangelist at *GoHarvesting.com*


I have read books on healing and miracles since the days of the charismatic renewal in the 1970's. I would strive to learn the rules and the correct words: any formula that worked. With Jonathan Brenneman's newest book, the reader will not find a new 7-point path to miracles. Instead, you will find your heart being transformed with a fresh passion and a fire within.

We need more books like this! This is inspiration; a fresh baptism of faith to see God move. If you are ready to step into the realm of the Spirit where the river flows with life and miracles, then read *The Mechanics of Miracles.*

Dr. Stan Newton – President *Crown Institute of Theology*

*The Mechanics of Miracles* is written in simple language by a man filled with wisdom, experience, and biblical knowledge. It breaks off many lies concerning relationship with the Holy Spirit and the life of a new creation man. It lists amazing miracles and shares Jonathan's walk to help us understand the glory of God and how we fit into all of this.

Although I have been very busy, I knew when he asked me to read it that it would be fruitful for me. It indeed has awakened perspectives in me that needed serious refining.

I highly recommend *The Mechanics of Miracles*. I believe that once you are done reading it, any confusion you might have about the spiritual life will be cleared up.

Shawn Hurley – Author of *He Sets the Prisoner Free.*
Founder *Happy Hands Ministry* and *Sarah's House.*
www.happyhandsministries.com


The *Mechanics of Miracles* is a treasure chest of rich nuggets of truth mixed with a legacy of experiential knowledge of God's character and nature. It's a Christ-centered masterpiece that will ignite and activate even the most skeptical or passive Christian into walking and talking like our King and older brother Jesus.

As someone who has seen the miraculous for decades, I have been inspired to raise the bar of my own expectations and grow into the son of God that Jesus has enabled me to be.

Kevin Peterson – Healing minister in Durban, South Africa

Jonathan is a true scholar. At age seven he began to read voraciously, devouring scriptures from Genesis to Revelation. He has also diligently studied moves of God and Holy Spirit revivals throughout history. Jonathan has researched innumerable eye witness accounts of absolute miracles – God's supernatural intervention on behalf of Christian believers everywhere.

However, it is not academic achievement that has propelled Jonathan into a lifestyle of practicing the presence of God and operating in signs, wonders and miracles. Rather, the Holy Spirit's move has carried him along this life path.

Jonathan teaches what he has learned through extensive study of scripture and following the Holy Spirit's leading. He relates how miracles are accessible and available for every born-again, Holy Spirit-filled believer.

Mrs. Arnolda Brenneman – Author, teacher, and president of *ARK (Artists Releasing the Kingdom) Ministries*; Lancaster, PA, USA.


God's heart is for miracles. They are windows into the Kingdom of God, revealing how God thinks and how he desires to show his love. Without miracles, Christianity risks becoming just another powerless religion, devoid of the Kingdom's demonstration. Miracles are essential for both believers and unbelievers, serving as glimpses into God's Kingdom.

*The Mechanics of Miracles* unveils the heart of God's Kingdom, which is rooted in miracles. This transformative book will challenge your theology and religious perceptions of God and his ways. It will reshape how you view the Kingdom of God and empower you to step out in faith, demonstrating the miraculous as a means for others to see and enter God's Kingdom.

Tom Scarrella – Evangelist www.SHAREtheFIRE.org

# Foreword

It just occurred to me that I have been friends with Jonathan Brenneman for several years now. Wow, time moves so quickly.

From the moment I met him, I was struck by his passionate love for the Lord and his willingness to step out in faith. Listening to his marvelous testimonies and miracle stories is a joy; he seems to witness Jesus doing amazing things almost every day.

There are many positive things I could say about Jonathan. He is a devoted husband and father. Jonathan loves the Word of God and the truth of who Jesus really is. On top of all that, he courageously ventures where many are hesitant to go—calling forth the glories of heaven in a foreign land.

In this era, many people speak about and write books on miracles. I probably have more than two dozen healing works on my shelf published in the last few years. Some of these works are quite good, but I don't think any of the authors have gone where Jonathan has gone. I would consider him an expert on this topic.

When he sent me a copy of his book, *The Mechanics of Miracles*, I knew I had to read it. I would describe it as an inspiring guidebook from one of the most gifted and knowledgeable men that I know.

I encourage you to reflect on every spiritual insight and practical paradigm that is revealed in this book. The truths that Jonathan packed in these pages are genuinely life-changing.

Jonathan challenges me to return to the apostolic mandate—to move in the power of the Holy Spirit and release the mercies of heaven here on earth. I am convinced that he will do the same for you. I believe *The*

*Mechanics of Miracles* will position you to step into your destiny and transform the world.

J.D. King, author of *Regeneration: A Complete History of Healing in the Christian Church.*
Jdking.net

# The Mechanics of Miracles

## Table of Contents

**Acknowledgements** ............................................. 7
**What People Are Saying** ................................... 9
**Foreword** ............................................................. 13
**1. God's New Normal for You** ........................... 1

*Let's Start from the Beginning* .......................... *1*
*Heaven's Abundance* ........................................... *6*
*God's Love Manifests in Power* ....................... *12*
*You Must Heal the Sick and Cast Out Demons to be a Disciple of Jesus* ........................................ *13*
*If You Honor Jesus, His Priorities Are Your Priorities* ........................................................... *16*
*Partially Preaching the Gospel Creates Resistance* ......................................................... *21*
*Humble Yourself* ................................................ *23*

**2. Demystifying How Miracles Happen** ........... 25

*The Basis for a Walk of Power* ........................ *25*
*Why I Hate When People Say "Jonathan Has a Spiritual Gift"* .................................................... *29*
*Varied Manifestations of God's Grace* ............ *30*
*Impartation* ........................................................ *33*
*We Need to De-Mystify the Working of God's Power Because the Need Is Overwhelming* ..... *36*

**3. Jesus Came in the Flesh** ................................ 39

*How Satan Opposes the Anointing* ................... *39*

*Why did Jesus Come as a Man?* ........................ 40
*How Do You See God?* ..................................... 41
*Let the Revelation of Jesus Challenge Your View of God* ........................................................... 43
*Beholding* ........................................................ 45
*Other Implications of the Incarnation* ............. 48

## 4. Metaphors to Explain the Mechanics of God's Power ................................................................ 51

*The Lightnings of Heaven* ............................... 51
*Sponges for God's Presence* ............................ 58
*A Hammer* ....................................................... 65
*Fire* .................................................................. 67
*A Sword* .......................................................... 68
*Rain And Snow* ............................................... 69
*God's River* ..................................................... 71

## 5. Jesus Was Crucified and Rose Again ........... 75

*Jesus' Torn Body Is Our Open Heaven* ........... 75
*There Is Only One Door* .................................. 77
*Jesus, the Seed God Sowed* ............................. 81
*Jesus' Death Means I Have Died* .................... 84
*Jesus' Death Broke Satan's Power and Freed Us from the Law of Sin and Death* ........................ 86
*Our Resurrection with Jesus Seats Us with Him in Heavenly Places* ............................................... 87
*Jesus' Death Reveals God's Love* .................... 89
*Go Against the Flow if You're Not Happy with the Religious Status-Quo* ....................................... 90

## 6. The Heart ...................................................... 95

*God's Garden* ................................................... 95
*The Weed of Disappointment* .......................... 96

*Communion with God* .......................................... *98*
*Waiting on the Lord and Fasting* .................... *100*
*Be Strong in the Lord and in the Strength of his Might* .................................................................. *103*
*Use your Tongue to Direct your Heart* .......... *106*
*Let God's Word Expand your Heart* .............. *107*
*I'm Gonna Explode* ........................................... *109*
*Promises for a Walk of Power* ....................... *109*
*Push to the Point of Failure* ........................... *111*
*A New Normal is a New Heart Reality* .......... *113*

## 7. The Mouth .................................................... 117

*Add your "Amen" to God's "Yes"* .................. *117*
*The Heart and Mouth Connection* .................. *118*
*Say What you Mean and Mean What you Say* *120*
*Exercising Authority* ........................................ *121*
*Immunity to Witchcraft* ..................................... *123*
*Fervency and Rest* ............................................ *126*
*Your Actions Must Accompany your Words* .. *129*
*Don't Just Minister out of Routine* ................. *130*
*The Heart-Mouth Cycle* ................................... *132*

## 8. God's Grace Manifests through Faith ....... 135

*Tongues and Interpretation* ............................. *135*
*Hearing, Feeling, and Seeing in the Spirit* ..... *138*
*Healing and Deliverance* ................................ *143*
*Power Phrases and Power Actions* ................ *147*
*Works of Power, Signs, and Angelic Manifestations* ................................................... *150*
*Greater Works* .................................................. *152*

## 9. God's Lightnings Flashing Through You .. 155

*There is So Much More* ................................... *155*

*Look for People who Want Jesus* .................... *156*
*Knowing Jesus and Making Him Known* ....... *159*

**About The Author** .............................................. **161**
**Heaven Now Missions** ....................................... **163**
**Contact** ................................................................ **165**
**Also By Jonathan Brenneman** ........................ **167**
**References** .......................................................... **169**

# 1. God's New Normal for You

## *Let's Start from the Beginning*

I want you to experience the tremendous spiritual abundance and riches that I now know. God has a supernatural "new normal" for you. To enter a new normal, the old has to die. Wisdom (the Lord) says in Proverbs 1:23, "Listen to my rebuke, and I will pour out my Spirit on you." Are you ready for a challenge?

When I speak of spiritual riches, I'm not talking about supernatural events in themselves. The supernatural in itself may be thrilling at first, but you get used to it. Experiencing God's glory is what drives me. If something is supernatural but doesn't have God's glory on it, I'm not interested. Before talking further about the dynamics of the spiritual world, I should review the foundational truths I'm starting from.

The true God is pure light[1] and love.[2] He is invisible,[3] but he is the source of all life[4] and knowing him is life.[5] God's glory is the weighty essence of who he is, especially his love, his power, and his sufficiency. It can be felt tangibly.

We have all sinned and fallen short of God's glory.[6] We've missed the mark, acting, thinking, and believing in a way contrary to who God is. That's what sin is. Being disconnected from the Source of life leads to death.[7] Some of us have had our own conceptions of "love," but it wasn't God's love and so it led to death. There is a way that seems right to people, but in the end, it leads to death.[8]

God sent his Son, Jesus, to rescue us from that vicious cycle of spiritual blindness, sin and death, to restore us to knowing him and experiencing his life.[9] We see the full and exact revelation of who the invisible God is in Jesus.[10] We would always be blind until sin and guilt were dealt with. We were never able to know God and his glory experientially until sin and guilt were removed.[11]

God removes sin and guilt by the spiritual principle of transference.[12] It works by faith. I once was with a wonderful group of Native Americans and prayed and saw Jesus heal dozens of them. Then a lady advised me, "What you are doing is wonderful, but you need to be careful because all of the sicknesses that you took off of these people can build up in your body and make you very sick. So, take the branch of this tree and transfer the sicknesses into it, so that you don't get sick."

I explained that I was not taking the sicknesses of the people or transferring them into my body, but that Jesus carried the sin and sickness of the world in his body.[13] She understood the spiritual principle of transference better than many Christians do! She just didn't understand yet what Jesus has done for us.

God didn't only transfer the problem. He dealt with it. When Jesus was crucified, what was killing us died with him.[14] Such love to rescue us from the miserable state we were in![15] But it was impossible for the Author of Life[16] to remain dead,[17] so he resurrected! By the spiritual principles of repentance and faith,[18] Jesus' death becomes our death[19] to that which was killing us, and his resurrection becomes our resurrection[20] into newness of life.

This message sounds crazy, so some ask, "How do you expect people to believe it? How do you expect people to believe that the Bible is saying the truth about Jesus?"

I've stopped trying to convince them. That is the Holy Spirit's job.[21] I know the message is true because it works. I feel the glory on it. I know what it has accomplished in my life. I feel God's love flowing through me like a river with peace, hope, and joy I could never have imagined.

I just share the message and the Holy Spirit convinces people. Sometimes a healing convinces them.[22] Many feel God's presence like a weighty cloud, a vibration in the

## 1. God's New Normal for You

atmosphere, or chills running through them when they hear it. Others might see a vision or start crying without knowing why. They are experiencing God's glory.

If you have not yet made that connection with God through Jesus, you can pray something like this: "Jesus, I've gone the way I thought was right, but I was wrong. I repent! Save me and change my life! I want to live in your light![23] I give you my heart, soul, and body." Then get baptized.[24] When you go under the water you are participating in Jesus' death, and when you come up, you are participating in his resurrection.[25] We are baptized into Jesus.[26] The heavenly inheritance and the promises are for Jesus,[27] and they are ours when we are baptized into Jesus.[28]

If you have already given your life to Jesus, you need to continue living by the power of the gospel message.[29] You may need to be reminded of it! The way you first made that connection with God is also how to continue in communion with him.[30]

Repentance is breaking communion with every spirit that was leading us to death, and then entering communion with the Holy Spirit.[31] Satan often appears as an angel of light.[32] Destructive spirits disguise themselves as benevolent.

Someone called me to help a guy who lived a few blocks away. He felt something choking him. It kept him from eating or drinking. He had barely eaten or drunk anything for the previous three days, but the doctors couldn't find any problem.

When I prayed for him and released God's goodness, he belched for a long time and then felt relieved. However, when I encouraged him to eat a banana, his throat closed again. I felt there was a spirit harming him that he had not broken communion with, so I asked him if there were any objects in his house that he wanted to get rid of.[33]

There were. One was a necklace given to him by a spiritual healing guru who was based just two hours from our city. People came from all over the world to see him, and miracles happened.

But the guru, called "João de Deus" or "John of God," wasn't of God. The supernatural works didn't have God's glory on them. They took people's attention away from Jesus, who is the radiance of God's glory.[34] They were like the cheese on a mousetrap. João is now in prison for running a large criminal organization, human trafficking, and decades of sexually abusing people who came to him for help.[35]

The man got rid of the necklace and several other charms, and the choking stopped. By getting rid of those charms, he broke communion with several spirits that he thought were helping him but really just wanted an opportunity to destroy him. He realized that the way he thought was right had almost led to his physical death.[36]

I have a friend who loved Yoga. She had heard that many poses were done in homage to Hindu deities, but she thought she could separate the exercise from the spiritual side of it. She nearly went insane and was then physically blinded by a spirit that she had unknowingly entered communion with as it tried to get her to throw herself out the window.[37]

I've had experiences praying a general prayer to release God's glory on a person who I didn't know anything about, and a spirit suddenly manifested or just left them. I didn't know the spiritual practices of the person before I prayed. I only found out later. It was a spirit the person had thought was beneficial. They thought it was light, but the true light of God's glory expelled it.

This is why it's important to test the spirits.[38] The only door to heaven and the only way we can connect to the true Source of Life is through Jesus,[39] so every spirit that truly is good directs people to Jesus and to what Jesus has done for us. God sends angels to minister to us.[40] I never invoke or pray to angels or any other spirits.[41] They come when I talk about Jesus. I put my trust in Jesus, not in angels,[42] but I thank God for angels. Holy angels worship Jesus[43] and would never want you to give them the attention or honor that Jesus deserves.[44]

Deceptive spirits are darkness disguised as light. They are fine with us giving them misplaced trust and attention to turn us from the light. Many people get a healing or financial blessing through them, but it is like the bait on a fishhook to

## 1. God's New Normal for You

cause them to connect with the spirit. Then when that connection is made, the spirit's true nature becomes evident, and the person has all kinds of problems that are much worse than the original one.

As I kept praying for people, I was surprised at how often evil spirits manifested and left their bodies when they were healed![45] The pain would intensify or move around their body as I rebuked it in Jesus' name. It finally had to leave, and sometimes did so with belches or some other manifestation. I would have thought it was just a natural pain! Some pains and problems are natural, but more than most people realize are caused by a spiritual issue.

Today, culture says that everything goes when it comes to sex, as long as everyone consents. But many people know from experience that isn't the case. Even people who aren't religious are on Reddit talking about how terrible they felt when using porn and how radically their lives changed for the better when they stopped.[46]

Many people suffering spiritual torment connected with the spirit tormenting them by having sex outside of God's design. It seemed right at the time, but the end was darkness.

The spiritual realm is much more real than most of us realize. Everybody has spiritual connections. You can be connected to the Holy Spirit through Jesus and the result is life. You can also be connected to spirits of darkness that lead to death.[47] Nobody is disconnected from the spiritual realm.

What is manifesting in your life? Is it the kingdom of God, which is righteousness, peace, and joy?[48] Or is it darkness? If you've done something that seemed right at first but was the way of death, repent now. It may have been having your palms read, going to a spiritual healer, trusting in charms or crystals, sexual activity outside of marriage, or something else. Break connection with that spirit, and by faith, connect with God through Jesus.

Real Christianity isn't about human ability or trying to follow a list of rules.[49] It is about breaking the old spiritual connections and making a new connection with God through

5

Jesus.[50] Then you let his Spirit manifest through you naturally![51]

If you haven't done so yet, ask God to baptize you in the Holy Spirit,[52] and then believe that you have received![53] Being baptized in the Holy Spirit is being inundated with God's presence. God promises that just as a father gives good gifts to his children, he will give the Holy Spirit to those who ask.[54]

Sometimes people are baptized in the Holy Spirit with great manifestation. Other people may not feel much at the moment, but later realize that something happened to them! I didn't feel anything and didn't start speaking in tongues when I received prayer to be baptized in the Holy Spirit. I thought I hadn't received, but I had! I realized it later. I don't even know exactly when I started speaking in tongues. I eventually realized it was God, not just gibberish.

## *Heaven's Abundance*

I grew up in a Christian family, but I was oppressed by the devil as a child. I thought of killing myself, but I was afraid that I would go to hell if God existed.

One day when I was about nine years old, I woke up with strong back pain. My mom said, "Why don't I pray for you?" I didn't expect anything to happen, but I felt a ball of energy start rolling up and down my spine until the pain was gone. That's how I became convinced that God exists.

I had a born-again experience[55] soon after, and was baptized in the Holy Spirit when I was 13. As a teenager, I decided that I wanted nothing more than to be a missionary and live for Jesus. I spent hours reading the Bible and books about prayer, fasting, missions, and revival. Sometimes, I didn't get home until 3 in the morning, because I was at a prayer event.

I had a few more tangible, supernatural experiences with God, but I had never prayed for someone and seen them healed through my hands. By the time I was 19 or 20, I felt frustrated with myself, frustrated with the church, and disappointed in

## 1. God's New Normal for You

God. I knew in my mind that God was good,[56] but in my heart, I felt that he'd been stingy with me.

That was when I went to a conference that changed my life. I wanted to lift my hands but it was so hard. When I finally did, I felt a vibration of God's glory start to manifest on my hands and spread all over my upper body until I was screaming and crying hysterically.

God spoke to me and said, "I'm generous![57] If I gave my son Jesus for you, how much more will I not also give you all things![58] I've never been stingy with you, and I've always wanted to do the miracles you've heard about, in your life.[59] The problem is that your lack of understanding has hindered you from experiencing all I have for you."

I needed correction! The first correction I received was when I became convinced from the biblical teaching at that conference that it is always God's will to heal.[60] No exceptions! It is just as much God's will to heal as it is to free people from sin! I started to see the invisible God through Jesus,[61] and a life of miracles began.

I've told the story in more detail in my other books, but to sum it up, since then I have experienced so many miracles that telling all of them would be like trying to tell you all the meals I've eaten for the last 20 years. I've experienced the generosity of God that scripture talks about. I often start weeping as I remember something Jesus did. Many memories bring me to tears. My eight-year-old daughter asks me to tell her stories of miracles until she falls asleep.

I can't even tell you the miracles I've seen Jesus do in the last week. But here are a few highlights:

- A lady beside me at the bus stop had a cast. She'd broken her arm 15 days earlier and it was still hurting a lot. I prayed for 15 seconds and all the pain was gone. She raised her arm and moved her hand with no pain.
- A lady had a steel plate and two pins that caused pain and hindered her from bending her knee. She also had

thrombosis in her leg. As I spoke, she felt a wind blow over her. The pain left and she bent her knee.

- I ran across the street to pray for a man with a crutch. He smelled terrible and his body looked so broken and crooked that it messed with my mind, but I let the presence of God in my heart challenge the unbelief in my mind. His leg was rotting without circulation and had an open wound. He said the lack of circulation saved him from dying by snakebite. In a few minutes all the pain was gone. He crossed the street to have coffee with us. As he kept talking, I kept releasing God's goodness on him. An hour later, as he was leaving, we noticed that he was carrying and swinging his crutch instead of leaning on it!

- As I prayed for a little girl, she said God put a box in her hand with a present. She felt it enter her hand and go up her arm into her body.

- A lady testified that she was healed of diabetes because she felt an incredible heat on her pancreas as we prayed. We are awaiting confirmation, but I also believe she is healed.

- A lady couldn't read or see clearly after a cataract surgery that went badly. God's power came on her head as heat, and she started reading!

- I had prayed for a lady in Malawi, Africa six months ago. A friend in the UK gave me her contact and I prayed by WhatsApp. She had a 4-centimeter brain tumor causing convulsions, and she went to South Africa in a wheelchair to have a surgery. This week I got the report of what happened. They scanned her brain before the surgery, and the tumor was gone! The doctors were shocked and cancelled the surgery. She stopped having seizures and returned to Malawi walking!

# 1. God's New Normal for You

I've sometimes been at the brink of tears for weeks on end, overwhelmed with Jesus' mighty works, feeling God's physically tangible glory as a weight of his goodness on my body, and currents of power flowing through me.

I've had supernatural winds[62] and rain in my house, as well as other unexplainable manifestations. I was talking with a guy on the phone the other day and he said, "Jonathan, when I talk to you it feels like there's a wind blowing through my body." Several people who have been healed have felt a wind blow over them.

On the street, the Lord has often showed me what a stranger's physical problems were and they were healed. Once the same thing happened when I saw a stranger's name on Facebook. When I go to a drug and alcohol recovery house or a new neighborhood, I often know several conditions that will be healed before I get there.

I've gone to poor neighborhoods in Brazil and raised my voice, asking who needed healing. Sometimes I've prayed for about half the people present and every single one was free from pain by the end...miracles one after another. I often come back from a local outreach and an hour later I'm crying because of what I just saw happen.

I can truly testify that God's mighty works are more than can be numbered.[63] If we tried to tell everything that Jesus did, all the books in the world would not be enough![64] Recently, I realized how many testimonies I don't even remember. I decided to go back on my Facebook wall to remind myself of some of the testimonies I had forgotten. Here are a few of the testimonies that I had posted in 2010, 12 years ago, and didn't even remember anymore:

- A friend in another state said his friend Gary was very sick and bedridden. We prayed on the phone. 10 minutes after we hung up, Gary called him and said, "I just felt a cool breeze blow over me, I got out of bed, and I'm fine now."

# The Mechanics of Miracles

- I prayed for a guy on the phone for his back pain. He went to the hospital, and they found a perfect spine. The steel rods were gone from his back!

- I was praying for a lady's speech impediment and an angel touched her hip. She hadn't told us that she had pain in her hip, but the Lord healed it. Another lady with Hepatitis C felt God's power come on her as heat and electricity.

- I prayed for a young guy with scoliosis. He felt nothing when we prayed, but when he sat down his spine started popping, and his back straightened.

- I visited a small church with 34 adults present. At least 15 people were healed by every indication we could tell at that moment. We couldn't find anybody who left with pain.

- A lady had a wound from an incision and physically felt it being stitched as we prayed.

- I prayed for someone who had broken her arm a week before. She took it out of the sling and started moving it in ways that were previously impossible, with no pain. She also moved her knee without pain, although she had a torn meniscus before that.

- A woman got set free from fibromyalgia pain and her husband from lower back pain.

- A person was freed from constant pain due to Lupus.

- The doctor was going to do a surgery on Friday. I prayed on the Sunday before the surgery. They found nothing wrong at the appointment on Monday and cancelled the surgery.

- I was talking about Jesus and a teenager's finger started to vibrate with God's power. He moved his finger up and touched his nose, which was hurting, and it was healed.

## 1. God's New Normal for You

- We visited a person late at night to pray. Pain went from level ten to zero, sight was restored to the eye, and he felt God touch his back and stomach.

- One of my housemates woke up to a strong smell of roses and the feeling that someone was looking down on him. Another housemate saw an angel downstairs.

- I had prayed for a neighbor who started to shake under God's power. A few months later, someone told me the neighbor gave his life to Christ and was speaking in tongues.

- I found out a person I had prayed for three years earlier was now out of his wheelchair.

- A kid broke two toes in the morning. At night we prayed and they were completely healed.

- A friend I'd been encouraging prayed and 9 cancerous lumps disappeared from someone's neck. He prayed for another person and a cataract disappeared.

- A lady with a hernia received prayer. She felt something like a hot coal behind the hernia, and the sensation that it was being sucked in. The hot coal remained and continued burning for several hours after we prayed.

Last year I heard the Lord shout, "I have a new normal for the church-that should have been normal all along! It's a 'normal' in which the church does the works of Jesus."

A life I could have barely imagined of power, glory, and experiencing God's generosity became my new normal after that conference. My whole perspective and way of thinking has been transformed. It's radically different.

Even if you've already been walking in God's power and seeing miracles through your hands, I want to encourage you to challenge every limitation and experience a new normal of a greater manifestation of God's Spirit through your life. God has no limitations![65] He can do more than we ask or imagine according to his power at work within us,[66] and he said that nothing is impossible for those who believe him![67]

## God's Love Manifests in Power

Many Christians accept various manifestations of God's grace such as prophecy and healing, but seem to think they are optional. Some say, "What really matters is love and having good character."

This false dichotomy between God's love and power is deeply unscriptural.[68] Throughout the Bible, God's love is manifest by his power.[69] What kind of love says the power to meet people's needs is unimportant? That's not real love at all![70] It's only in theory. Love without power is like faith without works. It's dead.[71]

God's love was manifested in power through Jesus.[72] Power makes God's love tangible.[73] I had been saved for years but when I began to see Jesus touch people in power, I felt like I had barely known who he was until then! I rarely saw people weeping because of God's love until I began to minister in power.

God's love manifests in power, and we see his love and nature through his tangible works of power. The Bible says the Kingdom of God isn't a matter of talk but of power.[74] Jesus said, "If you see me, you see the Father."[75] He revealed the Father's nature? How? God's compassion was manifest in the deeds of power that Jesus did.[76] If we lack the manifestation of God's power, we lack the revelation of God's nature.

One of the primary proofs that Jesus rose from the dead is that he continues to do the same works today as he did in the gospels. T. L. Osborne believed this and saw whole regions impacted by the gospel where ministers previously had no success. Jesus is alive today, and he is the same yesterday, today, and forever![77] The compassion that moved him to heal all the sick is still the same.[78]

1. God's New Normal for You

The Bible is the written Word of God, and it testifies to the Living Word of God, Jesus Christ.[79] What the Bible says was never supposed to be theory and word only.[80] The letter kills but the Spirit gives life.[81]

Jesus said the pharisees searched the scriptures but refused to come to him to have life, though the scriptures testified of him.[82] Jesus is the Word manifest in flesh,[83] manifest in power.[84] God's invisible nature was made visible in all that Jesus said and did.[85]

Jesus came full of grace and truth.[86] We have abundance of grace in Jesus.[87] That means overflow—more than enough grace for every need. The primary meaning of "grace" in the New Testament is power! We need the Holy Spirit's enablement to do what we can't do! We need God's grace to empower us to follow Jesus!

Jesus' incarnation is an essential truth of the gospel,[88] and we can't have the incarnation of God's invisible Spirit in flesh without power! Since the Church is the body of Christ,[89] Jesus has also come in our flesh.[90]

It doesn't seem so terrible if we say a church is lacking spiritual gifts. But the Greek language in 1 Corinthians 12 doesn't even mention "gifts" but speaks of "grace-effects," or manifestations of God's grace![91] How does it sound to say that a church is lacking the manifestations of God's grace? When we put it that way, we realize that power is not optional! Is God's grace manifesting in your life by the power of the Holy Spirit?

## *You Must Heal the Sick and Cast Out Demons to be a Disciple of Jesus*

When Jesus sent the disciples to evangelize, he told them to proclaim, "The kingdom of heaven is at hand."[92] Remember that the kingdom of God isn't a matter of talk, but of power![93] Jesus gave them power and authority to cast out demons and heal every kind of sickness and disease,[94] and he told them to heal the sick, cleanse the lepers, cast out demons, and raise the dead.[95]

In the great commission, Jesus told his disciples to make disciples of all nations, baptizing them and "commanding them to do everything I made known to you."[96] Jesus' teachings were for all future disciples. He never sent his disciples to evangelize without power.

A person can be saved without being a disciple. To be a disciple of Jesus, you must follow him and obey his commands. Jesus said, "As the Father sends me, I send you."[97] The Father sent Jesus to manifest his love and compassion in power to a dying world, and he sends us to do the same. The Father sent Jesus in power, and he sends us in power.[98] Disciples of Jesus go as Jesus went[99] and do what Jesus did.

Jesus said in the most emphatic language that those who believed in him would do the same works as he did, and even greater works.[100] He said that miraculous signs would follow those who believe, including healing the sick and casting out demons.[101] Jesus gave us the same glory that he himself received from the Father![102]

Jesus said, "He who has my commandments and keeps them, it is he who loves me. And he who loves me will be loved by my Father, and I will love him and manifest myself to him... If anyone loves me, he will keep my word; and my Father will love him, and we will come to him and make our home with him. He who does not love me does not keep my words; and the word which you hear is not mine but the Father's who sent me."[103]

How can we say, "I love you Jesus, but I'm not going to obey your commandments to heal the sick and cast out demons as I preach the gospel, because, well, those aren't my spiritual gifts?"

If you obey the commandments of Jesus to heal the sick and cast out demons, Jesus will come to you and manifest himself to you! How? You will see Jesus through what he does, and he will become more real to you than ever before.

# 1. God's New Normal for You

Have you ever heard of someone having a vision of Jesus that transformed their life? My grandmother did. She fell on the ground and Jesus came, eyes blazing with love, and brought her to the Father. She couldn't see the face of the Father on the throne because it was too bright, but he took her up on his lap like a little child and said, "I love you."

When she came back to the consciousness of this earth-realm, her face was radiant and she looked ten years younger. Her knees were healed. We could see that she had been with Jesus. If you've seen Jesus in his glory, your face becomes radiant and you reflect that glory.[104]

I've never had a vision like my grandmother did, but I've seen Jesus with the eyes of my heart and it has impacted me in the same way. His nature is revealed in his deeds. At times I can do nothing but cry because I see Jesus. He has manifested himself to me through healing and deliverance as I obeyed the command to heal the sick and cast out demons. I've seen Jesus' love and compassion manifested in his power.

You don't have to just hope that God might sovereignly give you an experience or a vision in which you meet Jesus. You can take a hold of the promise that if you obey Jesus' commandments, Jesus will come to you and make himself known to you. The book of Acts says that as the apostles preached the gospel, those watching took note that they had been with Jesus.[105] They spoke with heavenly wisdom and acted with heaven's power.[106] Would you like people to see that you have been with Jesus? Obey his commandments to heal the sick and cast out demons.

The church has so often ignored every part of Jesus' commission that we know we can't do in our natural, human strength, as if it were supposed to be possible without the empowerment of the Holy Spirit. "We can't heal the sick and cast out demons, but we can talk to people." We can't even do the preaching part without the empowerment of the Holy Spirit. How can we proclaim the gospel in power by our natural abilities? We need the Holy Spirit to empower us to do that just as much as we need his empowerment to heal the sick and cast out demons. We depend completely on him to do through us what we can't do in our own power as we obey the commission of Jesus.

## *If You Honor Jesus, His Priorities Are Your Priorities*

Jesus did as he saw the Father doing.[107] Healing and deliverance were high priority to Jesus because they were high priority to the Father. When the religious didn't want Jesus to heal on the Sabbath, he said, "She has been oppressed by Satan for 18 long years, so how can I wait another day to heal her?"[108] Jesus had an urgency about seeing her set free.

If we honor Jesus, we value what he values. If what is high priority to Jesus is low priority to us, we dishonor Jesus and dishonor God's word. Jesus is God's Word made flesh.[109]

What we value is manifest among us. If Christ's Spirit is not manifest in power, healing, and deliverance in the Church, it is because the Church does not value what God values and does not honor Christ. If we honor Christ, he manifests himself among us. If Jesus is our Lord, what is important to him is important to us!

Many Christians say they want revival, but they dishonor the Holy Spirit. When Jesus came, there were people crying out loudly,[110] falling to the ground,[111] the lame walking, the blind seeing,[112] the deaf hearing,[113] and evil spirits shrieking and fleeing.[114] Many church leaders are uncomfortable with that, because they lose control.

Some say, "We let the Holy Spirit move." Really? Does he need our permission? Or is he our Lord and we submit to him? What if we stopped thinking in terms of what we will let God do, and instead started thinking in terms of what he will let us do?

The Church of the Laodiceans thought they were rich, but they were poor, blind, and naked.[115] The qualifications some congregations use to consider themselves rich are really just dead, self-centered human religion, straw, hay, and stubble,[116] not eternal things. What religiosity values is worthless to God.

## 1. God's New Normal for You

Jesus talked about those who stored up treasures for themselves but were not rich towards God![117] The manifestation of Christ's Spirit among us is true wealth. How can we imagine that the Spirit of the Jesus the Bible testifies of will be manifest among us without healing and deliverance?

Paul rebuked the Corinthians for putting up with those who preached a "different gospel" and a "different Christ."[118] Without healing and deliverance, it's not the same gospel and it's not the same Jesus that the Bible tells us about!

I have noticed that the Greek New Testament has the same word translated "faith" and "faithful."[119] Men of faith are faithful to the revelation of God's nature in Jesus.[120] They are faithful to the Word God has spoken through Jesus,[121] including his will to heal and set the captives free.

Paul told Timothy to appoint faithful men who are able to teach others as leaders.[122] Obeying Jesus' commands to heal the sick and cast out demons, and being able to teach others to do so, are qualifications for elders. James instructed the church to call the elders to pray the prayer of faith, and the Lord would raise the sick man up.[123] How is a person qualified to be an elder in the church if he cannot fulfill the duty of an elder by praying the prayer of faith for the sick?

Immediately after affirming that Jesus is the same yesterday, today, and forever, the author of Hebrews warns not to be carried away by all kinds of strange teachings.[124] Someone who sees Jesus as different today than the Jesus we read about in the gospels has been carried away by strange teaching. That includes anyone who believes, "We read about Jesus being moved with compassion, healing all the sick, and casting out demons in the gospels, but we just don't see nearly as much of that happen today."

Beholding Jesus produces the same works in us, as we are his body here on earth. Of course, we are growing into the full measure of the stature of Christ, but we should at least be going in the right direction of beholding the same Jesus of whom the Bible testifies so that we can be transformed into his image.

If a person isn't even going in the right direction because his image of Jesus is different than the Jesus of the gospels, then how can he be a leader or an elder in the church? Paul exhorted the believers to imitate him as he imitated Christ.[125] But if a person is not imitating Jesus by doing what Jesus did, because they see Jesus as different today than he was in the gospels, how can we follow or imitate them without also being "carried away by strange teaching?"

Paul said he would speak of nothing but what Christ had accomplished through him in word and action, to bring the gentiles to obey God by signs and wonders, by the power of God's Spirit, so that he fully preached the gospel.[126] He didn't boast of what was possible with natural ability but of what Christ had done through him and of what was only possible by the power of God's Spirit. Bringing the gospel with word but not action is only partially preaching it.

Paul didn't come with eloquent speech. He came in weakness and trembling. His message and teaching were not with persuasive words of wisdom but with the demonstration of the Spirit and of power.[127] The letter kills, but the Spirit gives life.[128] God's kingdom is not a matter of words but of power.[129] The Spirit manifests God's word in power.

Paul told Titus that elders must hold fast to the faithful message.[130] According to Paul, preaching without signs and wonders was partially preaching the gospel, not fully preaching it.

Many Christians are listening to preachers who have eloquent speech, persuasive words, and human wisdom, but no power. They are impressed with these preachers' natural ability but not by what God has accomplished through them by his power.

Such preachers are not faithful to the gospel that Paul preached. Stop spending all your time listening to preachers with no power! They talk about what they don't understand, and their message lacks authority. Real understanding produces a manifestation. Preaching with authority flows from a life filled with Christ, and the preacher is living what he's talking about!

## 1. God's New Normal for You

The people marveled at Jesus' teaching because he taught with authority, not as the scribes and Pharisees.[131] They saw the authority in Jesus' teaching by what he did. If there's no power for miracles and deliverance, the message also lacks power to set people free from sin. The wisdom of man is foolishness to God.[132] Human wisdom may sound impressive, but it lacks authority.

Peter said elders are to be examples to the flock.[133] They should be examples of following Jesus, and Jesus commanded his disciples to heal the sick and cast out demons. How can you be an elder (church leader) if you are not first a disciple?

Jesus told the disciples they would preach the gospel to all nations, but first to wait in the city until they were clothed with power from on high![134] Power is not an option. It is essential for preaching the gospel.

If you are a leader and thinking, "You're saying I'm not qualified to be a leader and I'm not even a disciple of Jesus," don't be offended! Rather, just repent. Obey Jesus' command to heal the sick and cast out demons. Make his priorities your priorities. This is a great opportunity to humble yourself. If you do, you will receive God's grace,[135] and Jesus Christ will come to you!

I'm not saying that people who aren't walking in God's power never have anything good to offer. I highly value scholarship, including understanding the original languages and the historical and cultural context in which scripture was written. Some of the scholarship I value even comes from cessationists.

Even so, don't look to someone who is not obeying the commands of Jesus to teach you to be a disciple of Jesus! Many people consume their time and energy on mere words, theory, and religion that values human ability and human wisdom rather than valuing that which only God can do and his power manifest in our weakness.

Merely human religion eats up so much of Christians' time and energy that it hinders many Christians from knowing Jesus intimately and obeying him. Last year I heard the Lord say,

"You can't give your all for religion and give your all for Jesus."

Merely human religion often makes heavy demands on people's time, loyalty, and resources, and that stops them from ever becoming disciples of Jesus. What the religious organization is demanding is not always what Jesus is asking of you. Many people have sat in church for decades, endlessly learning but never coming to a knowledge of the truth![136] They want to hear another good message, but it is so hard to get them to act and to obey Christ!

Many people's energy is consumed by charismatic churches that use carrot-and-stick legalism to keep people doing what they want. The stick represents threats of punishment, and the carrot represents rewards. The miraculous is accepted doctrinally but lacking in practice, and it's used as the carrot dangled in front of people to win their devotion or get them to put more money in the offering.

People caught in such systems usually have little real expectation. If we preach that God gives us his Spirit and does miracles among us because we believe, not because of the works of the law,[137] then we have a real abundance of miracles, not just empty talk about them.

Am I challenging you? I'm writing to build up and strengthen the church, not to tear it down. However, some tearing is involved in the process of becoming strong. The muscles tear when one pushes the limits of their strength. A weight lifter loves a challenge. There's no growth or change without a challenge. There's no growth without some tearing of what is weak so that it grows back stronger.

Rather than making excuses for powerlessness, let God's word challenge you. And challenge your own unbelief! If you're going to experience the new normal God has for the church, you must challenge what you have thought was normal until now and stop letting your expectations be defined by past experience.

## 1. God's New Normal for You

# *Partially Preaching the Gospel Creates Resistance*

Scripture warns us of those who have a form of godliness but deny its power.[138] Scientists produce a weakened, partial, or dead form of a pathogen to cause resistance and create an inoculation. A weakened or partial form of the gospel also creates resistance against God's work.

Some regions still have many people who've never heard the gospel. Those who follow Christ often face severe persecution. For some, to be baptized is to risk their lives. Christians are beaten, their houses are burned, their possessions taken, and they are ostracized from society.

If you visit such a region, ask people how they came to know Christ. Nearly all of their conversion stories involve a dream or vision of Jesus, a healing, or a deliverance from demons. In some churches, you can't find a Christian whose conversion doesn't involve a supernatural encounter with God's power.

In other regions, many people have been constantly exposed to some form of Christianity. It's on the radio, on TV, on billboards, everywhere. They've gone to church. Family members are Christians. However, the form of Christianity that people are exposed to is often weakened, compromised, and adulterated.

Jesus warned us against the leaven of the Pharisees and of Herod.[139] Leaven in scripture often refers to legalism and religion based on human effort instead of God's grace and empowerment.[140] Jesus said we are the salt of the earth, but if the salt loses its saltiness, what good is it?[141] This referred to the dishonest practice of selling salt mixed with sand.

If the form of godliness that people are exposed to lacks power, it creates resistance. People think, "I've already tried that," "It doesn't seem to be working so well for my family," or, "I don't want to be like them!"

Preaching a weakened or mixed form of the gospel results in a post-Christian society. Much of Europe is considered post-

Christian, and the United States and Latin America are in danger of becoming post-Christian societies if we do not return to a pure and powerful gospel message.

Our friend Reinhard planted a church with several hundred people in post-Christian Austria, in an area considered a graveyard for church planters. A church that size was huge for a congregation in Austria. What did they do? They went out on the streets ministering healing. The only way to get through in the post-Christian culture was with a gospel of power.

Preaching a form of godliness that denies its power often leads to syncretism with the occult. Mel Tari shared that many of the people in his cessationist church resorted to consulting witch doctors when they had a problem.[142] A lady in another city contacted me last night and confessed that she had resorted to witchcraft when in a desperate situation. She didn't find help, so a family member gave her my number and she asked me for prayer. Why wasn't the church the first place she would go for help?

I recently returned from a mission trip to Marajó, a large island at the mouth of the Amazon River, with about 10,000 villages which are still unreached with the gospel. Where the church has gone, it has sometimes done much harm by imposing its religiosity instead of simply preaching Jesus and the gospel. We learned that a certain witch doctor has much influence in the region; even many church people go to him when they need to be healed. When the church failed to preach Christ the healer, the people sought another spirit that deceptively offered to meet their needs.

So many young people today go to a university and reject the faith of their parents. They received a weakened version of Christianity that created resistance. The youth that tend to keep their faith as adults are those who have experienced God's power, and especially those who have seen Jesus heal someone through their own hands.

Some Christians emphasize getting people to pray a salvation prayer so they can get their ticket into heaven. Nothing is wrong with using a salvation prayer as an

## 1. God's New Normal for You

evangelistic tool. However, people often repeat a prayer without even understanding the gospel message so that they can believe in their hearts. Many people sitting in churches have prayed a prayer for conversion but still don't understand the basics of the gospel!

Scripture says that if you confess with your mouth that Jesus is Lord AND believe in your heart that God has raised him from the dead, you will be saved.[143] Salvation from a scriptural standpoint is much more than just a ticket into heaven! It is redemption in every area, healing, deliverance, and restoration to communion with God so that we can reflect who he is!

The Pharisees crossed earth and sea to make a single convert, and then turned that convert into twice the child of hell that they were![144] Jesus didn't say to make converts. He said to make disciples.[145]

Our focus must be lives transformed, not just how many people we can get to raise their hands and repeat a prayer! If we preach a weakened, powerless, diluted form of the gospel, we end up working in opposition to the transformation God wants to bring!

## *Humble Yourself*

If this chapter about the need for God's power has challenged you to realize how far your current experience is from what the gospel looks like, humble yourself and cry out to the Lord. Help Jesus!

I want you to see your need for the Holy Spirit and your helplessness without him. Some people might think I'm a strong Christian, being astounded by the stories of miracles that I share. On the contrary, I often feel I'm a weak Christian! I have so much room to grow, and I need God's help!

Just as I cried out to the Lord years ago to save my soul and deliver me from sin, I often cry aloud to Jesus now. I cry out for his work in other people's situations just as I cried out when I needed to be delivered. I can't keep going without his empowerment! I weep and plead in tongues. However, this pleading is a cry of faith, not of unbelief. I know that I call and God answers me![146]

When God delivers the person I'm praying for, it's like he is delivering me again. I've failed many times on my own strength to see a person healed or delivered. I've failed many times on my own strength to share the gospel in power. We are insufficient of ourselves to do anything, but God delivers us and qualifies us as ministers of the New Covenant![147]

# 2. Demystifying How Miracles Happen

## *The Basis for a Walk of Power*

Around 2005 or 2006, I began posting testimonies on a social media site called Xanga. After that, Myspace was the big craze and I shared testimonies there. Then Facebook exploded and I started sharing testimonies there. Through that, I connected with many likeminded people. I probably have a few hundred Facebook friends who walk in God's power in their daily lives. I know how they think differently than the religious status-quo, and I know how my thinking has changed.

I often physically feel God's glory on my body. Dozens of times it has been as tangible as if I were swimming in water. I've perceived what has triggered God's glory to manifest in that way. I have had so many experiences with healing, angelic activity, signs and wonders, and God's glory manifesting tangibly that I have observed how these supernatural events happened, and I've connected those observations to what scripture says.

I've also learned to recognize common sayings and beliefs that hinder the church from walking in God's power. I've written several books and hundreds of articles over the years, sharing how God has corrected my thinking and the miracles that have happened as the result of that correction.

The basis for the supernatural that I've experienced is not anything new or mysterious. It is through understanding the simple truths of Jesus' incarnation, death, and resurrection.

## The Mechanics of Miracles

These truths are so simple they are hidden from the wise and learned and revealed to babes.[148]

It's easy to say we agree with good theological statements about Jesus' incarnation, death, and resurrection, yet act as if they were not true! All the keys I will share with you revolve around simple gospel truths. The power is in the gospel.[149]

I've been working to see this new normal established in the church. I'm sharing with Christians who have never seen a miracle in their life, getting them to lay hands on the sick, explaining how it works, and miracles are happening through their hands. Nowadays, it's much more exciting to get someone who has never seen a miracle to minister than it is when I myself lay hands on a person and they are healed.

I have a message that produces power. I've seen the tremendous results in the lives of those who receive, understand, and act on this message. They begin to live an abundant life of miracles. Other Christians have seen the miracles when I prayed and sometimes ask questions. I've often explained how it works over hamburgers. Those who understand and act on that understanding experience miracles.

Last year I was invited to a small city in the state of São Paulo, Brazil, to do a *Heaven Now Seminar*. It was based on my *Heaven Now* books series. The first session was a teaching consolidated from my book *Present Access to Heaven*. It talks about what Jesus' death and resurrection mean for us. The second was based on my book *I Will Awaken the Dawn*, which is about praise and proclamation. The third was based on *Jesus Has Come in the Flesh*, which talks about Jesus' incarnation. The fourth session was answering common questions and encouraging the people to persevere and act on these truths.

I physically felt God's glory and wept as I wrote each one of the books in the *Heaven Now* series. God's glory also manifested through his word as I taught the seminar. In the second session several people were spontaneously healed during the message before even receiving prayer. Then I began to have the people minister to each other.

## 2. Demystifying How Miracles Happen

Einstein said, "Insanity is continuing to do the same thing and expecting different results." I taught the people to pray in a different way to get different results. By the end of the seminar, we only found one person present who had any pain, and it was reduced by 80%.

I was recently invited to speak in several small churches in São Paulo state again this year. The purpose burning in my heart was not to just have a healing service in which I would pray for everyone, but to see this new normal that God has for the church established by getting the believers to begin doing the works of Jesus. Yet I only had one session to speak to these groups! The previous year I had taught four sessions, and even that was a consolidated form of the teaching! Now in one session I had to summarize the most powerful truths that were going to change these Christians' lives so that they would start to experience Jesus' supernatural works.

In the largest of those churches, I spoke about how the invisible Spirit of God is revealed in Jesus and manifest in this earth-realm through the body of Christ, the church. Although I could have shared testimonies for days on end, I kept the testimonies to a minimum and gave them just enough to raise their expectation and understand how abundant this new normal is that God has for the church. I didn't open my Bible and read every verse for time's sake, but my statements were loaded with scriptural references.

I taught them simply how to pray in a different way to get different results, and they ministered to each other two times. Many people were healed. Then I asked, "If you are here and still feel pain in your body, raise your hand." Nobody raised their hand. I asked them to make sure, to press where it hurt before, to move their bodies. Nobody was left with pain!

More than once, a young guy has seen the miracles Jesus did on an outreach and asked me later, "Hey, how does that work?" I explained when we went out for burgers after the outreach, and they were soon seeing Jesus do miracles. One of our guys, José, is an ex-atheist and had given his life to Jesus three months before I taught him to minister healing. He recently prayed, and a blind man's vision was restored! He has also prayed for a person who got up out of a wheelchair, a lady who was healed of stage-four cancer, and a young man in our men's group who had HIV and tested negative after prayer.

On the way back from one mission, I learned that a young lady in the car with us was suffering with various conditions, including severe pain and bleeding from the uterus. The doctors had told her repeatedly that she could not have children and needed to remove her uterus. Yet she had refused the surgery because she wanted a miracle. She was engaged to a young man, and they wanted children.

I and another missionary prayed for her on the way home. She felt heat, and the pain left. She went to the doctor that week and he said "Nothing is wrong with you. You can have 10 children if you want to."

The next weekend, she and José prayed for a lady whose foot was shriveled and paralyzed after three surgeries. The woman limped around, walking on only the toes of that foot, suffering severe "level 10" pain and cramping in her leg and back, daily taking 150 milligrams of pain medication. As they prayed for her, the pain left and she started to move her toes. After about half an hour of receiving prayer, she was walking normally, with the full range of motion, foot flat on the floor, and no pain. The only sign that anything had ever been wrong was the scar on her ankle. I cried a lot on that mission!

Just a few weeks ago, another young guy asked me "how it works" as we ate burgers after a mission. I explained a few of the points I cover in this book. The next day he prayed, and a man got out of a wheelchair.

This book is based on my experience of trying to consolidate the message to share as much as possible to help you without the detailed studies I've done in other books and articles. I only cover some points briefly even though I took many years to understand them, because they are foundational for further insights.

I'm not quoting every relevant scripture, but what I am saying is loaded with references to scripture. Scriptures I refer to are found in the endnotes. I want you to get the big picture

## 2. Demystifying How Miracles Happen

and find some keys to help you start walking in this new normal that God has for the church!

## *Why I Hate When People Say "Jonathan Has a Spiritual Gift"*

Many other Christians, when they see the miracles in my life, say, "Jonathan has a spiritual gift." I tell them, "No I don't!"

Christians often disqualify themselves from what is available to all of us because they think of it as a "spiritual gift," which they assume they don't have. <u>The first way this happens is that the idea of a "spiritual gift" distracts them from the revelation of Jesus.</u> They have the same Jesus that I do.

Healing, prophecy, and miracles are manifestations of the Spirit of Jesus. They are God's love in action. Jesus was moved with compassion and healed them all.[150] Compassion manifested in power. God's actions contain revelation of his nature. One of the ways we see Jesus is through his mighty works. When people's focus is on a supposed special superpower that someone has, they miss the revelation of Jesus.

Seeing God's glory in the face of Jesus[151] transforms people's lives. It results in praise to God which produces an increasing manifestation of God's glory. I want people to see Jesus through the miracles so their lives are transformed and Jesus is glorified.

I saw Jesus through the healings at that conference, and it changed my life forever. Even though I had been saved, I felt like I had previously barely known who Jesus was. Scripture teaches that we can grow in the knowledge of God.[152] I read the gospels and wept, thinking, "How didn't I see this before? Jesus healed them because of his compassion!" The name of Jesus brings tears to my eyes because I have seen what he does. The testimonies fill my heart. When I say that Name, it means something wonderful to me!

The miracles in my life flow out of the revelation of Jesus. If other Christians see Jesus through his works in my life, that revelation produces the same works and miracles through their lives.

Second, focusing on a "spiritual gift" keeps people from seeing that they have the same promises of scripture that I do.[153] The miracles in my life are firmly based on scriptural promises and basic gospel truths that are accessible to all of us.

Third, focusing on a "spiritual gift" makes the way God's kingdom manifests on earth seem mysterious. There is a way that spiritual things work and God's invisible Spirit manifests visibly on the earth. There are spiritual principles of cause and effect which work for everyone. I call these the mechanics of miracles.

I want other Christians to catch the revelation of Jesus through the miracles they see in my life. I want them to understand the gospel revelation and the promises of scripture that have produced power in my life. I want them to understand how miracles happen. However, if they are focused on a "spiritual gift," they don't have ears to hear[154] or a heart to understand that this life of abundance in Christ is for them too!

## *Varied Manifestations of God's Grace*

I don't believe in spiritual gifts in the sense that most people think of them, as if they were special superpowers distributed to certain people. The word "gifts" in 1st Corinthians 12:1 isn't in the original text. It was added by translators in an attempt to clarify, but the translators' attempt to clarify has instead brought a lot of confusion.[155]

Paul wrote in 1 Corinthians 12:1 that he didn't want the Corinthians to be ignorant about spiritual things. I want you to understand the cause and effect of the supernatural so that God's invisible Spirit will be manifest tangibly through you. The change in perspective will transform your experience. It's so simple that it's hidden from the wise and learned![156]

In the rest of 1 Corinthians chapters 12 and 14, what is translated "spiritual gifts" is simply "grace-effects" in Greek.[157] I've read those chapters in Greek, and it now seems

## 2. Demystifying How Miracles Happen

absurd that the text could have been interpreted as talking about special superpowers distributed arbitrarily to different people.

To put it simply, the passage is talking about different manifestations of God's grace through different people in the context of a meeting. Paul was giving instructions for a church meeting and talking about what they were doing at the moment, not about what they were capable of or not capable of. Not everyone does the same thing at the same time, and God manifests his grace through multiple members of his body. Our meetings aren't supposed to be one-man shows. The "grace-effects" are not special superpowers that Christians receive apart from or in addition to receiving the Spirit of Christ.[158] Rather, each individual manifestation, healing, prophecy, miracle, and word is a "grace-effect" of the same Spirit.

I have studied this extensively, including cross-references and the Greek grammar used in related texts, and I've written about it in several articles on my blog.[159] The list of "grace-effects" in 1 Corinthians 12 is a menu of some of what is available to you in Christ. I've experienced all of those "grace-effects" in my life. The experience of many people who walk in the supernatural is that if they start in one area, such as prophecy or healing, all the other manifestations of God's grace start to flow through them as well.

That doesn't mean that one person will always do everything. We each have the fullness of Christ's Spirit dwelling in us, but Christ's ministry has been divided among us.

When you're on the street and a need is in front of you, you have what that person needs because you have Jesus and all the fullness of God dwells in him. God can manifest his grace in whatever way is needed through you. But when you're in a meeting with other Christians, God desires to manifest his grace through various members of his body. He doesn't want to do it all only through you.

Although there are different particular manifestations of God's grace, the most basic mechanics of how the supernatural manifestations happen are the same. The same river of God that heals the sick also brings forth prophecy and drives out demons. The empowerment to live a godly life is also in that river. It's the same source and the same river. Stop thinking in terms of "spiritual gifts" and start thinking in terms of God's river flowing through you. Jesus said that rivers of living water would flow from the one who believes in him.[160]

God's love flows through me and reveals what people's problems are. I often look at someone, see where they have a problem in their body, speak God's word, and they are healed. The same river enables me to love my enemies and produces every other manifestation of God's grace. People think it's a gift, but it's just the river of God's love flowing from heaven! Rather than trying to obtain some "spiritual gift," be filled with the Holy Spirit and let the river flow!

When we read our Bible translations, it tends to sound like 1 Corinthians 12 is talking about special superpowers separate and distinct from the Spirit of Christ that we all receive. That idea is not in the Greek text. The teaching of Jesus himself, long before 1 Corinthians 12, is clear that healing, deliverance, tongues, supernatural wisdom, and works of power are for all Christ-followers.

Scripture has promises that any Christian can take a hold of related to every one of the grace-effects listed in 1 Corinthians 12. Walking in each one of them can be taught, learned, and practiced. Anyone who has been baptized in the Holy Spirit can heal the sick, prophesy, speak in tongues, and so on.[161]

Yes, some people excel in different areas. That is because they have grown in experience with the Lord, sensitivity, faith, and practice in that area, not because they have a special superpower that other Christians don't have! All the manifestations of God's grace come from the same Spirit, the Spirit of Christ!

Rather than focusing on "spiritual gifts," I want to help you focus on the promises of scripture, the person of Jesus, and the message of the gospel as it relates to a supernatural life of power.

## 2. Demystifying How Miracles Happen

Mark Hemans preached, "I was pastoring a church and I said, 'Lord, nothing is happening. No one is getting saved. No one is getting healed. Nothing is happening. Is there a better way of doing this?' And the Lord said to me, "If you will preach me, I will come and do the work. With that, I had a revelation of who Jesus is, that forever changed my life. I realized that the ministry was not about me. It didn't depend on what I felt, or what gifting or anointing. It wasn't about me. I grew up in the charismatic movement in the 1970s and I was taught about the spiritual gifts and the anointing, and I thought it was about what I had. But when he (The Lord) spoke to me I realized that he was sufficient. If he would only come; and he would do the work. I had a revelation of Jesus. It is Jesus among us who heals, who delivers, who speaks, who saves, who changes lives. It's got nothing to do with me. Hallelujah!"[162]

Preach Jesus! Honor Jesus! Call on Jesus, and Jesus will come!

## *Impartation*

I started living a life of miracles at a conference held by Global Awakening, Randy Clark's organization. As some of you may know, impartation is one of the primary focuses of Randy's teaching. I've seen and experienced it. It's real and biblical.

You may be surprised that I don't believe in "spiritual gifts" in the sense that most people think of them, but I do believe in impartation. Some truths in scripture seem on the surface to contradict each other, but when our understanding grows, we realize that they really are not contradictory. The promises of God and the truth of what we all have available in Christ may seem on the surface to contradict the concept of impartation. In reality, both truths work together.

Among those who minister in God's power, there tend to be two camps. One emphasizes impartation, words of knowledge, angels, and various manifestations. The other emphasizes faith, God's word, and God's promises.

## The Mechanics of Miracles

Sometimes people in one camp go as far as rejecting those in the other camp because the mindsets seem to be contradictory. Some who emphasize faith have rejected impartation with the laying on of hands.

It may be difficult to understand how the truth that we have spiritual riches and fullness in Christ is coherent with the Bible's teaching about the laying on of hands and impartation. But consider that Jesus, being God, was strengthened by angels.[163] In the same way, we can receive strengthening, empowerment, and encouragement by the Holy Spirit through the laying on of hands.

I emphasize faith and God's promises. I have seen miracle after miracle by just taking hold of God's promises and acting. My mindset is, "I have Jesus, so I have everything! I have Jesus, so I have what the person in front of me needs, whether I feel like it or not, so I'm going to give it to them." The person may be in a wheelchair or look really bad, but I let my actions and the presence of God in my heart confront the unbelief in my mind.

Just a few months ago, I prayed for a guy I saw in a wheelchair at the bus stop and he got up and walked without pain. I didn't feel a special "anointing" or leading. I just acted on God-facts and the promises of scripture. I am rich because I have Jesus, so I'm going to give away those riches to the world. I could tell one story after another of miracles that happened by simply acting like that.

We have been given fullness in Christ,[164] but there is more![165] It's all available to us, but we can live in and walk in much more than what we have experienced so far. We are growing in the knowledge of God.[166] We must continue to be filled with the Holy Spirit.[167] The evidence that one is filled is the overflow of heavenly riches. The Holy Spirit reveals to us what God has freely given us[168] so we can walk in it.

Once Randy Clark prayed for me and it felt like God reached in, grabbed my stomach, and turned it inside of me. Since then, I have wept a lot more. Did Christ dwell in me before that? Yes. His compassion was the same before. But

## 2. Demystifying How Miracles Happen

Jesus' compassion became more of an experiential reality to me through impartation. I was gripped with God's compassion in a stronger way than I ever had been before.

Impartation is precious. I often pray for people and they feel the weight of God's glory on their hands as a sign to encourage them to act in faith. This last weekend I saw many people weeping as they felt Jesus' compassion for others. It was precious and holy.

However, people who misunderstand what impartation is sometimes ignore God's promises and gospel facts about what we have in Christ because they think they haven't received enough impartation. Then they don't act based on God-facts. When a person in a wheelchair is in front of them, instead of confronting their own unbelief and acting in faith, they think, "I still need more of God before I can help that person."

Many people also ignore God's promises because they think they don't have that spiritual gift. If your understanding of impartation and "spiritual gifts" causes you to discount the scriptural promises of God concerning what you have in Christ, then you don't understand impartation or "spiritual gifts" accurately.

People also often disqualify themselves because they feel that they need more anointing. They often use the word "anointing" in a way quite different than scripture does! I have frequently been in situations on the street or in someone's house where people wouldn't say they felt "the anointing" or a "good atmosphere," but I act aggressively in faith and suddenly people are being healed and tangibly feeling God's glory. As I learned from Dan Mohler, ambassadors of Christ[169] are the thermostat, here to set the temperature, not the thermometer to measure it!

It seems that some people's concept of the anointing has become separated from Christ, whose name means the Anointed One. We are in Christ. We are called "Christians." The word "anointed" is in the very meaning of the name.

In some circles, I hear people talk about receiving the anointing of this person or that person more than they say the name of Jesus. When you understand what I'm saying, your focus won't be on the anointing of this or that person anymore, but you will focus on Jesus and on the promises of God that are all "yes and amen" in him.[170] Those promises far surpass the "anointing" of any particular person. Receive and value impartation, but focus on Jesus, not on the vessel!

Let's simplify things and turn our attention to the person of Jesus, the power in the gospel message, and the promises of God which are all "yes and amen" for us in Christ. Receive impartation with the laying on of hands to help you walk in that. Be filled with the Holy Spirit. He will manifest through you that which you possess because Jesus lives in you. Receive impartation and also act on God's promises

## *We Need to De-Mystify the Working of God's Power Because the Need Is Overwhelming*

I don't have special superpowers. Even Jesus could do nothing of himself but had to rely on the Father just as we do.[171] What I experience seems extraordinary to many Christians, but my experience is different than theirs because I think differently than they do. Because I think differently, I act differently and I get different results.

If they would think and act in a similar way as I do, they would get similar results. Real heart beliefs manifest in actions.

"Insanity is continuing to do the same thing and expecting different results." Unfortunately, many Christians keep praying, thinking, and acting in the same way and hoping for different results. Then when nothing changes, they say, "That must not be my spiritual gift." People's results change when they learn to think and act differently.

I weep as I'm overwhelmed with God's goodness and generosity. I also weep because I know the need and it is so overwhelming. Jesus said that the harvest is plentiful but the laborers are few.[172] I see a person healed of a condition such as a brain tumor and think of how many other people in my city have similar conditions. Jesus is the answer, but how can I take Jesus to all of them?

## 2. Demystifying How Miracles Happen

The need is enormous! It's far too much for me alone, but most of the church doesn't even know what they have in Christ! I don't want other Christians to look at me and think I have a spiritual gift that they don't have. I want them to understand the message and power of the gospel, and jump into the harvest with me!

This book is partly a plea for help. The world is hungry. The harvest is ripe. We have the Bread of life[173] and the riches of heaven[174] to give to needy people. God is no respecter of persons.[175] He is generous to all who call on his name.[176] He can do more through your life than you could ever ask or think![177] There are no limits. Nothing is impossible for God,[178] and nothing is impossible for him who believes![179]

# 3. Jesus Came in the Flesh

## *How Satan Opposes the Anointing*

The fact that Jesus came as God in a man's body is one of the essential doctrines of the Christian faith.[180] Many Christians accept this doctrine on the surface but act and think as if the implications of it weren't true.

God's invisible Spirit and our tangible realm come together in Jesus' incarnation. The incarnation is foundational for walking in the anointing. The very name "Christ," found in the word "Christian," means "anointed." Walking in the anointing should be normal for Christians.

Scripture says the antichrist spirit denies Jesus' incarnation.[181] It opposes the anointing by convincing Christians to think as if Jesus never came in the flesh, and that hinders them from living a normal Christian life of doing the works of Jesus.[182] Then what should be normal seems extraordinary to us, and what we think is normal is really subnormal. Wherever powerlessness is found in the church, an antichrist spirit has influence.

The good news is that when we recognize the lies of the antichrist spirit and stop agreeing with them, we start experiencing the "normal" God has for the church of walking in the anointing and doing the works of Jesus.

To break agreement with the antichrist spirit's lies, we must first understand why Jesus came as a man and what that truth implies for us.

## *Why did Jesus Come as a Man?*

In the beginning, God created the world and said it was good,[183] and he created mankind and said it was very good.[184] He put mankind in the Garden of Eden[185] and gave him dominion over creation.[186] Scripture says that the heavens are the Lord's, but the earth he has given to the sons of men.[187] God's intention was that his dominion would be extended throughout the earth through mankind walking in communion with him.

Jesus told us that God is Spirit,[188] and scripture tells us repeatedly that God is invisible.[189] Yet the invisible God made visible man in his image and likeness.[190] God then gave mankind dominion over this visible realm. This was so God's invisible nature would be manifest on the earth through people fellowshipping with the Holy Spirit.

This is one of the major keys to understanding spiritual dynamics. Spirits are generally invisible, but they manifest in bodies through the agreement of people. God's intention was that he would be seen through people. The Holy Spirit seeks people who will enter into partnership with him. Angels act when people speak and act in agreement with God. Demons also seek the agreement and partnership of people. God gave dominion over the earth not to angels but to mankind.[191]

Hebrews says that God crowned mankind with glory and honor, putting all things under his feet. Many translations say it like this: God gave mankind control over everything. (On the earth)[192]

If I give you the keys to a car and you crash it, who was controlling the car? Was I still controlling it? God is all-powerful and all-knowing but not all-controlling. The beliefs that God controls everything that happens and that everything is pre-determined to happen for a reason are not scriptural. Those ideas come straight from Greek philosophy and from the gnostic cult that denied Jesus came in the flesh![193]

God's purpose was that his invisible nature would be manifest visibly on the earth through mankind, who he created

## 3. Jesus Came in the Flesh

in his image and likeness. But all men sinned and fell short of God's glory![194] The Old Testament tells us that God looked for someone to stand in the gap, but he found no man, so he stretched out his own hand.[195]

God's purposes and the thoughts of his heart stand through all generations.[196] Because his purpose for mankind never changed, God never retracted the dominion over the earth that he gave to mankind. When he saw that all men had sinned, God stretched out his own hand by coming as a man!

## *How Do You See God?*

Job cried out and wished he could approach God face to face, as to a man.[197] Jesus is the answer to Job's cry! Although God had reached out in various ways to reveal himself, he was still invisible and mysterious until Jesus came. John tells us that nobody had ever seen God, but Jesus made him known![198]

Jesus is the perfect image of the invisible God,[199] and he said that if we see him, we see the Father.[200] He is Emmanuel, meaning, "God with us."[201] Because of Jesus' incarnation, God is no longer far, mysterious, and unknowable, as depicted by the Greek philosophers and in so many other religions.

Death came into the world not through God's will or permission, but through mankind. Redemption came through the man, Jesus Christ. People who receive God's abundance of grace and the free gift of righteousness now exercise dominion in life through the man, Jesus.[202] Redeemed people, cleansed from sin by the blood of Jesus and restored to communion with God, may once again reflect God's glory, image, and likeness.

Jesus said that eternal life is knowing God![203] Salvation from a biblical perspective is about so much more than escaping hell and going to heaven. It is about once again being able to see God as he is, walk in communion with him, and reflect who he is.

Most people still have a distorted perspective of the invisible God because they try to see him through sinful man that has fallen short of his glory, instead of through the sinless man, Jesus Christ. They try to see God through life, through disappointments, and through what people have done. Yet if we could see God as he is through life, scripture would never say, "Nobody has seen God" and Jesus would not have needed to come to reveal what God is like.

If we've been told that God is in control in the sense of everything that happens having been planned by him, we tend to see God through life's experiences rather than through Jesus. The most common question that leads people into atheism is, "If God is real, why did he allow that to happen?"

I've heard a rape victim say, "God must have had a reason for allowing this," and a lady who'd been sold into prostitution, "I just thought that was what God had for my life." These are extreme examples, but many people think like that.

I have seen demons manifest and come out of people with loud belches when they understand that God is not controlling everything that happens. Evil spirits latch on to the lie that "God did that" or "God allowed that and he didn't protect you," and they whisper, "If God is good, then why did that happen?"

Scripture says we look not at things that are seen but at things that are unseen.[204] Faith knows all that is seen was created by God's invisible word.[205]

Jesus is the invisible Word of God made visible in flesh, heaven manifest on earth. All God's promises are "yes and amen" in him. The "yes" comes from God and the "amen" comes from man.[206] God's "yes" is established in heaven. The "amen" of a man establishes it on earth. Jesus came as God and man, so God's "yes" and man's "amen" are united in him.

Jesus said to pray, "Your kingdom come on earth as in heaven."[207] However, many people assume God controls everything, so they believe that whatever they see happen on earth must be the manifestation of God's will. They try to see the invisible God and know his will through the situations they see in a broken world instead of looking at him through Jesus and seeing in Christ the invisible heavenly reality of God's glory, manifest in flesh.

## 3. Jesus Came in the Flesh

To believe for God's power to change any situation, you need a revelation of God's will that contrasts with the natural visible reality. You have to see the invisible.[208] God has revealed his will in Christ.[209]

If you think every visible reality was either caused or allowed by God and thus reveals God's will, you have no revelation of God's will to challenge what you see. Such thinking makes it impossible for you to know the invisible God, be convinced of his will, see the unseen, or have faith for miracles.

If you think God either caused or permitted a sickness, how will you believe him to heal it? If you think God is the one who allowed the sickness, how will your heart comprehend the compassion[210] of the invisible God whose nature is to heal?[211]

If God were controlling everything that happens, then everything that happens would be a reflection of who he is, because God's nature is manifest in his actions. If God were controlling everything, Jesus would not have had to come as a man.

To be clear, God's eternal purposes are firm and unmovable.[212] The devil isn't a threat to him and isn't going to stop him! So, if you say, "God is in control" in the sense of how things end in the course of history, I agree with you. He is the victor and we have victory in him![213] His eternal purposes will surely be fulfilled. However, the way God has chosen to fulfil his purposes is not by controlling every detail on the way. Rather, it is by creating mankind in his image; giving man dominion on the earth; sending Jesus as a sinless man when all men had sinned, and now, by redeeming man through Jesus.

## *Let the Revelation of Jesus Challenge Your View of God*

If you're going to experience the new normal that God has for you, you have to let go of the old. You have to let the revelation of God's nature through Jesus Christ challenge the way you saw God when you had a distorted view of him through your life and experiences.

Has somebody done something terrible to you? Have you ever asked, "Why did God allow that?" God is the defender of the weak.[214] It's his very nature as revealed in scripture. God isn't in heaven giving permission for child-abusers and rapists to act. His nature is to protect the helpless and rescue the oppressed, but he is invisible. He is looking for people to enter into partnership with him to protect the innocent so that his invisible nature is manifest visibly on earth.

Did you have a father who was cold, distant, or harsh? It probably affected your view of God. But that was a reflection of your father's brokenness, not of what God is like!

Have you asked, "Why didn't God heal that person?" God's very nature is to heal. It's one of his names. But God is invisible. He is looking for people, in communion with him, to release his word and power to heal the sick!

Isaiah 53 teaches that Jesus carried our pains and sicknesses.[215] Matthew 8:17 quotes Isaiah 53 and makes it clear that Isaiah 53 speaks of physical pains and sicknesses. Yet we turn the "Yes"[216] God has spoken through his Son[217] into a "Maybe," listening to the voice of the serpent saying as he said to Eve in the garden, "Has God really said…?"[218] We hear songs and theology referring to God healing the "sicknesses and diseases of the heart," spiritualizing the promise of scripture in unbelief. That diluted and powerless gospel lacks even the power to deal with the pains of the heart, because it presents an image of another Jesus who lacks the compassion of the Biblical Jesus.

Even people deeply involved in healing ministry may ask, "Why wasn't that person healed?" and it often hinders them. I've heard people in healing ministry say that healing of a certain condition is a "rare miracle" because we haven't heard of it happening much.

We would never have even started healing ministry if we hadn't learned to look to Jesus and see the unseen. It's so easy to fall back into letting what we have or haven't seen create our

## 3. Jesus Came in the Flesh

expectation, instead of letting God's glory in the face of Jesus[219] create our expectation.

Metal rods and plates disappearing from people's bodies used to be almost unheard of. Now it happens all the time. We are increasingly hearing testimonies of people healed of schizophrenia, bipolar disorder, and autism. Even for those who are already ministering healing, look to Jesus and let God's glory that you see in him challenge everything you feel is normal.

I want what is normal to Jesus to be normal to me. I let the revelation of Jesus challenge my unbelief and challenge what I feel is "normal" all the time. Do you know any Christian on earth who no longer needs to grow in the knowledge of the Lord, in faith, in love, in purity, in power, and in reflecting Jesus through their life? I don't!

It's not that God didn't heal. It's that we didn't see God's invisible nature manifest visibly through human beings in that situation. Everyone who came to Jesus was healed, and everyone who touched him was healed.[220] If Jesus comes to that person in front of you, what do you expect to happen?

But if you see Jesus with the eyes of your heart[221] and his Spirit manifests through you, then Jesus is coming to the person in front of you and they will see and experience Jesus through you. The church is the body of Christ.[222] God is an invisible spirit, but he is seen and manifest tangibly in a body.

## *Beholding*

The church is often ignorant about spiritual things. People involved in various other religions, the New Age, and witchcraft often understand the mechanics of spiritual things better than many Christians do, but they are deceived. They are deceived by evil spirits that disguise themselves as angels of light,[223] and they do not see that Jesus is the only way to the Father.[224]

However, they do learn how to connect with spirits. Spirits are invisible but look for a body to manifest in. People involved in spiritist religions connect with spirits through an image, often an idol. They connect with a spirit, and then learn to open themselves up to that invisible spirit so it manifests through them tangibly. We've seen how destructive the results of that are!

Christians know that Jesus is Lord and every spirit that is from God glorifies Jesus.[225] He is the only door and the only way to the Father. Yet many Christians don't understand the spiritual principles by which the invisible world affects this visible world, including the principles by which people connect with spirits and those spirits manifest through them.

Both the occult and God's kingdom operate spiritually. I don't recommend studying demons or looking for hidden knowledge outside of the Bible. I'm not encouraging the occult. I'm explaining how the spiritual realm works.

If people don't open themselves up to the Holy Spirit, they will form other spiritual connections that are destructive. I want you to connect with the Holy Spirit, and the only way is through Jesus Christ. Anything else is dangerous!

Pagans connect with evil spirits by beholding images. We connect with God's Spirit by beholding the image of God in Jesus Christ.[226] Scripture says we look not at what is seen, but at what is unseen, for the things that are seen are temporary, but what is unseen is eternal.[227] We can see the unseen by looking at Jesus.

How do we see Jesus? The first way is reading the Bible. The whole Bible testifies of Jesus[228] and points to him. We ask the Holy Spirit to open the eyes of our hearts to see Jesus, and he makes the scriptures burn in our hearts.[229] We also see him through his mighty works in people's lives today. We see Jesus through testimonies. Praise and thanksgiving are like spiritual eyes with which you can look at Jesus.

Those who worship idols become like them,[230] but when we behold God's glory in the face of Jesus[231] we are transformed into the same image, glory to glory,[232] and become like him. The invisible Spirit of God, which was made visible in Jesus, is then manifest in us.

## 3. Jesus Came in the Flesh

People must know the nature of a spirit to have communion with it so that it manifests through them. Many Christians don't even know who Jesus is, because men have annulled God's word by their tradition.[233] It's so simple. Jesus was filled with compassion and healed them all.[234]

If our image of Jesus is distorted by religious traditions, what we are beholding is not an accurate reflection of God's nature. That hinders us from having communion with the Holy Spirit. If we lack communion with the Holy Spirit because our image of God is distorted, then we lack the Holy Spirit's manifestation through our lives. Then we are left with godless religiosity in which we try to do what seems right, rather than living by grace. Living by grace is yielding to the Holy Spirit and allowing him to manifest his nature through us by his power.

If what is manifesting in our lives doesn't look like Jesus, it shows that the image we have of God is distorted. It has been formed by looking at something other than Jesus, or having a view of Jesus that is distorted by religious traditions and different than the Jesus we read about in the gospels.

Sin distorts our image of God, but the blood of Jesus deals with sin so that we can once again see God as he is, know him, and walk in communion with him. Salvation is a spiritual connection to God who is invisible, and communion with him by which the river of life from heaven flows through us.

God revealed his will in Christ. Leading up to his statement that Jesus is the image of the invisible God, the apostle Paul prayed that the Colossians would be filled with the knowledge of God's will in all spiritual wisdom and understanding so that they would walk worthy of the Lord, fully pleasing to him, being fruitful in every good work, increasing in the knowledge of God, strengthened with all might, with all patience and longsuffering with joy, giving thanks to the Father.[235]

Many Christians think as if God's will were a mystery, which is to think as if Jesus never came in the flesh. They are trying to see the invisible God through life and not through Christ. The result is the opposite of what Colossians says.

Because they are not convinced of God's will, they lack understanding and are always asking, "Why?" They are unable to walk worthy of the Lord, fully pleasing him, or be fruitful in every good work. Faith pleases God,[236] but faith is impossible without knowing what God's will is. As long as faith is lacking, they are never fruitful in every good work. Neither will they increase in the knowledge of God if what they are looking at is life rather than the revelation of God's will and nature in Christ.

The revelation of God's will in Christ strengthens us with power in our innermost beings, but Christians who are not filled with the knowledge of God's will are weak, always struggling. Because nothing makes sense to them, patience, longsuffering, joy, and thanksgiving are lacking.

This diagnosis is probably the primary cause of powerlessness in the church.

## *Other Implications of the Incarnation*

Several other implications of the incarnation relate to walking in God's power. Satan's lies contradict these truths and hinder Christians from walking in God's power.

I preached a sermon at a drug and alcohol recovery house on the weakness of Jesus. You ask, "What kind of message is that?" It's actually a key to walking in God's power!

Jesus became like us in every way, but without sin.[237] He never stopped being God, just also became fully human. He is not a high priest unable to sympathize with our weaknesses, but rather was tempted in every way as we are.[238] He was hungry,[239] weak,[240] tired,[241] and suffered as a man.[242] He received ministry from angels[243] and from other people.[244] Jesus said he could do nothing of himself, but only as he saw the Father doing.[245]

Jesus has always been fully God, but he didn't do miracles just because he was God. He did miracles as a man with every weakness that we have, but in perfect communion with the

## 3. Jesus Came in the Flesh

Father. He is our model, and scripture tells us to imitate[246] and follow him.[247]

If Jesus were only able to do his works and live as he did because he had some superpower that we don't have, then we would never be able to do the same works that he said we would do.[248] Yet many Christians still think as if Jesus did miracles only because he was God. That's clearly contrary to what scripture teaches. Jesus could do nothing of himself and had to depend on the Father just as much as we do, to do anything![249]

Another implication of the incarnation is that the body and the physical world are important to God. Gnostic sects denied that Jesus came in the flesh because they held to a false dichotomy between the spiritual and physical. It is the same false dichotomy held by many whose doctrine removes provision for physical healing from salvation and teaches that it is only spiritual![250]

The incarnation shows us our responsibility for God's will to be accomplished. Jesus came as a man because God gave responsibility to men. We are the body of Christ and we have a responsibility to preach the gospel, heal the sick, cast out demons, cleanse the lepers, and raise the dead.[251] If it's not happening it's not because God isn't doing it! It's because the body is not staying firmly connected to Christ the head[252] and obeying him!

# 4. Metaphors to Explain the Mechanics of God's Power

## *The Lightnings of Heaven*

Electricity in the atmosphere, like God's Spirit, is invisible. Ice crystals and warm water droplets create static electricity when they move together in clouds. The clouds become electrically charged.

A cloud is part of a giant capacitor. Capacitors are common components of electrical devices. They become charged with electricity and then release it in an instant. They have two charged plates with an insulator in between. The cloud is one plate in this giant capacitor. The ground is the other plate, and the atmosphere in between is the insulator.

"Capacitance" is the amount of electrical energy that a capacitor stores. Capacitance can be increased in three ways: by increasing the size of the plates, moving the plates closer together, or increasing the insulation.[253]

In a similar way, our capacity for becoming charged with God's power can increase. Increasing the size of the plates is like being edified by the Holy Spirit through God's word. Walking in close communion with God is like moving the plates closer together. Increasing the insulation between the plates is confronting increasingly difficult situations by the power of the Holy Spirit.

The negative charge at the bottom of a cloud pushes away negatively charged molecules on the ground, causing it to acquire a positive charge. The strength of the charge begins to create a conductive path by creating streamers of ionized air coming down from the cloud. The strong electrical charge also causes things on the earth (including the human body) to send up streamers of positive charges.

Finally, the ionized air meets a streamer, creating a conductive path, and we see lightning! We hear a shock wave called "thunder" and an incredible amount of heat is released. This is the tangible manifestation of what was invisible up to that point.[254]

You are the cloud. You are a capacitor, and you get charged through communion with God. If you unite yourself to the Lord, you become one with him in Spirit.[255] Your spirit and his Spirit move together like the droplets in a cloud rubbing against each other. This is being strengthened in our innermost beings by the power of the Holy Spirit.[256] The apostle Paul talked about God's energy at work within him![257]

At times, I have felt power flowing like currents from my hands! More frequently now, I feel currents flowing from my heart. I don't know how to explain it well because it's not a physical sensation like power flowing from the hands is. I recognize God's power going into the person as it is happening. Whether or not you physically feel power is not the measure of how charged your heart has become with God's Spirit. However, sometimes you may feel the power physically. If Jesus lives in you, you have access to all the power of God in him!

We can learn several principles from the analogy of lightning:

### 1) Different degrees of conductivity and power
If you stick your tongue on a 9-volt battery, you'll feel a shock! But that 9-volt battery isn't typically going to arc through the air. The energy is carried by a conductor, and there are different degrees of conductivity. However, when a very strong charge builds up, the power creates its own conductive path.

This is important to understand. Some people are more receptive to God's Spirit, and some people are less receptive. But as you become charged with the Holy Spirit, the strength

## 4. Metaphors to Explain the Mechanics of God's Power

of that charge will often create its own path. Even people who are resistant, clearly in unbelief, and hostile to God get struck by the lightnings of heaven.

I have seen this personally on many occasions, and I can share many stories from my own life as well as others'. Bradford McClendon had terminal cancer and he wanted to die! God destroyed that cancer in a Benny Hinn meeting. Even his atheist doctors acknowledged that the disappearance of the cancer was supernatural, but Brad was furious at God for healing him! He finally repented and responded to God's goodness a year later.[258]

I recall a teenage girl at a meeting who didn't even want to be there, but her mother made her go. She turned her back to the man prophesying to her, but God's power came on her, delivered her, and brought her to repentance!

Many times, after praying and weeping at home, I felt like my heart was going to burst with God's presence. I thought, "Someone is going to be healed!" As I was walking down the street or going about my life after that, I prayed for someone on the way who had no expectation of a miracle. However, God's goodness compelled me to be aggressive against the person's affliction, the power created its own path, and I saw the person healed.

People in need of healing or deliverance have often been set free after a word of knowledge concerning how they fell into bondage, a need to forgive, or some other key piece of information. This created the conductive path for God's power to touch them. If God gives you a word of knowledge, step out with it!

Because of such experiences, some create an expectation that "hindrances to healing" such as unforgiveness, unbelief, or bitterness will stop God's power. I've often seen this mindset cause people to forget broad and incredible promises of God such as, "If you believe, nothing will be impossible for you."[259] Complicating the simple truths of God's word can be the greatest hindrance to faith!

If you believe that the unforgiveness, unbelief, or issues of the person receiving will stop God's power, it will kill your faith and you won't see those people healed. Reinhard Bonnke told the story of a lady in a wheelchair who was in complete and utter unbelief and God told him, "I'm going to heal her!" She was healed, and the experience challenged Reinhard's paradigm.[260] To enter the new normal that God has for you, your paradigm needs to be challenged!

This is a major area of controversy among some healing ministers, but let's simplify it. Repentance, forgiveness, and God's work in a person's soul are certainly essential. A person may receive physical healing when they forgive. In that case, God's power flows through the soul to the body.

God's power can also flow through the body to touch the soul. A person may be unrepentant, unbelieving, and bitter, but God's power heals their body. Through the healing of the body, God's goodness touches the soul bringing them to repentance.

I don't disagree with healing ministers who talk about the importance of forgiveness. I'm just saying it happens both ways, so follow the Holy Spirit's leading. If you have a word of knowledge that someone needs to forgive, go with it! But don't let such issues limit you regarding who you believe God can touch! Follow the Holy Spirit, not formulas.

Jesus said if you believe, nothing will be impossible for you.[261] He didn't say if those you lay hands on and pray for believe, nothing will be impossible for you. The strongest scriptural point on this is that everyone who touched Jesus was healed.[262]

Remember that Jesus had every weakness we have and could do nothing of himself, but had to rely on the Father, just as we do. If all who touched Jesus were healed, nobody touched him and it didn't work because they needed a counseling session. What was possible for Jesus is possible for us.

A person may become so charged with God's Spirit that the power creates its own path of conductivity. Yes, sometimes mountains and obstacles stand in the way, but Psalms says that the mountains melt like wax before the presence of the Lord.[263]

## 4. Metaphors to Explain the Mechanics of God's Power

It takes a little heat to melt wax or ice, and a lot of heat to melt steel or stone.

This aspect of the mechanics of miracles is important to understand. God is all powerful, but since he works on the earth through people, there are varying degrees of the manifestation of his power, presence, and glory. Instead of giving up or coming up with explanations that contradict God's promises to explain why you didn't see something happen, keep turning up the heat! In the chapters on the heart and the mouth, we'll talk about how to do that.

We are like the cloud in the lightning metaphor, but we may also be like the object on the ground that receives the lightning strike. The strong charge at the bottom of the cloud forms streamers of ionized air rising from objects on the ground, creating a conductive path reaching up for the lightning to strike.

In the same way, when you keep exposing yourself to God's Spirit, meditating on his word, stepping out in faith, and filling your heart with testimonies, it changes you so that you become like a lightning rod for the Holy Spirit. It forms a hunger in you that won't be satisfied with anything less. I often just start crying because of what I've seen God do, and I want to see it again. I want to see the manifestation of God's Spirit, so I'll look for someone in pain. People who have that hunger step out in faith, and that gives opportunity for the lightnings of heaven to strike.

Maybe you minister on the street and pray for every person you see in a wheelchair, but you still haven't seen anybody get up and walk. However, your hunger and act of faith of going up to pray for that person is forming something in the spiritual realm that may be invisible but is real, like those streamers of ionized air reaching up as a conductive path for the lightning.

Several scripture passages refer to God purifying people like gold or silver.[264] Isn't it interesting that gold and silver are some of the best conductors of electricity! The redemptive work of the Holy Spirit in your life can increase your conductivity for his power!

**2) Seeing the invisible**

The Bible says we look at things that are unseen, not what is seen.[265] It's so easy to think that nothing happened when you prayed for someone and didn't see anything happen. I don't think that way anymore. I've learned from experience to discern what I don't see. The electricity is real and is there before you see the manifestation of that power when lightning strikes.

I can't tell you how many times the following scenario has taken place. I prayed for someone, often someone on the street who had no faith or expectation, and saw no change happen naturally. However, I felt God's power being released in my heart. My heart was now growling inside and saying, "Jesus is Lord!" How did I feel that power released through my heart? I don't know how to explain it, but it's something I've developed with experience. What I felt in my heart was so real that I wasn't even considering what I didn't see happen naturally.

I prayed for the next person in the same way and saw heaven's lightnings flash! The invisible reality I felt in my heart when I prayed for the first person led to a tangible manifestation the second time. It was not that nothing was happening the first time. The cloud became so charged up with God's power the first time when I acted in bold faith that the second time the charge created its own conductive path and broke through all resistance.

Sometimes I have approached several people before seeing the lightning flash. I was at an outreach giving soup to people living on the street in Goiania, and over the course of time I approached several people and asked if they had a need for healing.

Most of them said they didn't, and the ones who did had conditions that couldn't be immediately tested. Spiritually, my heart was burning so I kept confronting the lying feeling that nothing was happening. The charge in my heart kept growing until I felt it was going to explode.

When we were almost finished, I found a guy sitting on the curb. Half of his body was in severe pain because a car had

## 4. Metaphors to Explain the Mechanics of God's Power

hit him. I touched him and commanded the pain to go, and immediately it was gone from his arm. I continued hammering with God's word, feeling heaven flowing from my heart until all the pain was gone from the rest of his body.

He kept getting up and down, sitting and standing, raising his arm to show what he could do with no pain. Suddenly, he was mute in God's glory and couldn't even speak for a while, but only cried. We saw the lightnings of heaven! Other people present were healed quickly, one after another. The air was thick and heavy with God's glory. That's what I love!

With bold words of faith, let God's presence burning in your heart confront everything contrary that you see and feel around you. Then the charge builds until heaven's lightnings flash! I speak so boldly that people around me could easily think I'm crazy or out of touch with reality. And then I keep going regardless of natural conditions!

I don't care what people think anymore! They haven't seen what I've seen, and they don't know what I know. Jesus' opinion is what matters.

### 3) Persevering

If you understand what is happening spiritually; how an incredible charge of God's power is increasing, even if you haven't seen the lightning yet, you'll no longer say, "It didn't work," and you won't quit so easily!

Many Christians who don't understand spiritual dynamics give up before they see heaven's lightning's flash. God's power was already being released when they started, but they didn't realize or discern it, so they stopped.

I just prayed for a little girl on my way through the park. I choose to look at Jesus and be more impressed with who he is than with the breathing tube or the way the body is disfigured. Real faith is a heart belief put into action. Many people think they have faith, but they have just given mental assent to doctrine without putting it into action, so it's fruitless.

I exercise faith when I say, "I'd like to pray for you," and command the body to be whole. When you consistently make that choice to act and confront the conditions you come across, you are forming something in your heart. If you don't give up, the result of what you have cultivated in your heart will be more than you could have asked or imagined. It's like that electrical charge building and the air becoming ionized until that invisible reality manifests tangibly.

Many of the people I know who walk in God's power just started acting and persevered. They prayed for everyone they could. Some of them didn't see anybody healed for quite a while. However, something significant was happening. They were learning to love people. Heaven's reality was being formed in their hearts and it eventually bore much fruit.

## *Sponges for God's Presence*

I often speak aggressively like this when ministering: "May your body become like a sponge for God's presence right now, in Jesus' name! God, thank you for your glory inundating every part of their being! In Jesus' name, God's glory filling everything, driving out everything that's not in heaven! No place for disease or torment!"

Many people are healed, and sometimes this causes demons to manifest. If that happens, I continue, thanking God and saying, "Turn up the heat Lord!" Demons and sickness can't stand it anymore and they have to go.

I also say, "I release the weight of God's glory on you in Jesus' name!" We have access to God's glory in Jesus. In the last year, I heard a certain man had attempted suicide. I found an excuse to go to the apartment by praying for a little girl first. God's presence was like a force field around the child, her mom felt it standing six feet away, and the girl's lungs were healed.

I was going to ask if anyone else would accept prayer, but the man asked for prayer himself. I didn't know much about him, yet I prayed to release God's goodness as a weight on him.

He fell backwards in the couch, his eyes fixed like he was no longer there, and his eyelids started fluttering. He got very hot. You could feel the heat radiating off of him as you got

## 4. Metaphors to Explain the Mechanics of God's Power

close. I was shouting thanks to God and saying, "More God! Thank you for your goodness on him! Turn up the heat! No place for anything that is hurting him! Let your presence drive it all out!"

He fell forward from the couch to the floor, crawling on his hands and knees. He crawled to the bedroom and threw a big bag of witchcraft articles at my feet. He then crawled to another closet and threw another stash on the floor. We figured he realized they were harming him, so we put them in a big bucket and threw them all away.

He crawled back to the living room, stood up, and a spirit of rage manifested. It screamed, "He's mine! I'm going to kill you!" It tried to punch me, but couldn't hurt me. His flailing fists barely touched my shoulders and stopped. I laughed and said, "Do you think God's love is going to stop pursuing him? Your time is up! Get out now!" He collapsed on the floor.

When he got up, he didn't know what had happened! He didn't know that he had pulled all those witchcraft articles out of the closet. Then I understood what happened. It was the spirits themselves, controlling his body, which crawled over and gave up the items that were attaching them to him. It was as if they were surrendering and saying, "We can't stand this anymore! Here are our things. We'll go now." We explained what happened, and he prayed with me to receive Christ.

I persisted in releasing God's presence into that man. The more God's presence came on him, the more it displaced the evil spirits and torment. All of that wouldn't have happened if I had just prayed once and stopped. We inundate people with God's presence. God's word carries his presence.

It's common to pray several times and each time, the pain gets less until it is gone, or a tumor shrinks until it can't be found anymore. Often, a person who has cancer pain feels all the pain leave, but we must keep inundating them with God's presence until the tumors are also gone. We don't want to just leave them half-saturated, but fully-saturated so that no more room is left for disease. It's not about God deciding to answer or not. It's about God's presence, which dwells in us, being released through our words, our hands, and our faith into them.

# The Mechanics of Miracles

Once in a while, we've had experiences in which God's power came on a person and they were healed, but they regressed. Vision was restored, deafness was gone, or pain was gone. But some days later, the problem returned. In other cases, there was definite improvement but we never saw 100%. I prayed for a woman and all the pain left, but the cyst was still there. I saw her again three months later. She was still pain-free, but still had the cyst. I prayed for her again and it disappeared. Those experiences aren't the norm, but they have happened.

People with the "God is in control" mentality can't understand any of this. They tend to pray one time and then leave it up to God to answer. They say, "God doesn't do things half-way." If the person still feels pain, they assume God said, "no" or it wasn't his time. Instead of persisting in faith, they say, "We asked, and now it's up to God." They are quick to assume "it didn't work."

God isn't playing games with us. His nature is to heal, but his Spirit is invisible and there is a way that God's invisible Spirit is released through us. God doesn't do a halfway job. However, sometimes we need to persist in releasing his Spirit until everything else is completely displaced.

The sponge analogy reminds us that there are different degrees of saturation. Some materials are also more absorbent than others. Some take more time to soak up the water. A sponge will absorb water quickly, while a piece of wood will take much longer. The deeper you submerge a material, the greater the pressure and the less time it will take to become saturated with water.

A pastor had hearing aids. We ministered and I could tell that he quickly assumed it wasn't "working" when he didn't notice any immediate change. I've often talked to people who thought like that. I tell them that it's common to persevere and see great miracles, so I want to pray more. He was thinking of healing as something God does or doesn't do, rather than understanding that there are mechanics to how God's power is released.

## 4. Metaphors to Explain the Mechanics of God's Power

It took a little tenacity and perseverance to get started, but soon many people were being healed there. There was a lady who'd had a botched cataract surgery and couldn't read or see clearly. God's power came on her as a tremendous heat. People around who put their hands near her felt like they were sticking their hands into an oven. The pain from another issue left her body, and someone showed her a card. She could read the regular print! But she still had trouble reading the fine print.

I rejoiced and was going to keep going, thanking God, stretching my hand out, and speaking God's word. It's common for a person to get better, but not 100% yet, and we keep soaking them until it is 100%. But the pastor interrupted!

He got all excited, but at the same time he wanted to make sure it was real. He was frantically pushing the card in front of her face, asking her to try to read the small print again. I saw that she felt pressured and stressed because she couldn't read the fine print yet!

Pressuring her to keep trying to read the fine print when she just tried was totally interrupting what God was doing! In the spiritual realm, it was opposition to God's work because it was an attempt to get the focus off of Jesus and God's word which was manifesting God's glory on her. God's power was all over her like fire, and of course we were going to give her the chance to read the fine print again…but after we kept thanking God and soaking her with his goodness for a few more minutes!

I have seen that Satan tries to get people to unwittingly interrupt what God is doing and get the focus off of Jesus. And I've seen Jesus glorified in many such situations by being assertive and sometimes just plain stubborn.

One night I went to a local mountain where people pray and joined up with a group of people. They were prophesying that an old lady would be healed. It saddened me because it was just religious, creating the worst kind of unbelief. Instead of exercising authority to release God's power and asking the person to test the condition, they perpetually put God's promise off to some indefinite time in the future. If it's always "tomorrow," it's never now!

## The Mechanics of Miracles

After they finished, I saw that the old lady was limping badly. Her son was helping her walk. I asked if I could pray for her. She said I could, but as if she didn't expect me to pray right then and there.

I stretched my hand towards her knee and commanded, "In Jesus' name, pain go now! Thank you, Holy Spirit, for glorifying Jesus by touching her." I asked her how it felt now and she immediately responded, "Oh, I'm sure it will get better. Thank you." It was a typical religious response from a person who had been so disappointed by powerless religion that talks about healing but doesn't expect anything to happen!

It reminded me of a Pentecostal woman in Rio de Janeiro who covered her mouth in shock when she bent down and touched her toes with no pain in her back. In spite of all the jumping and shouting and yelling in tongues, she did not expect to be healed by Jesus that night! Praying for the sick was just another religious ritual and everyone would always say, "It will get better" or, "I am healed by Jesus' stripes" without daring to test it!

I said, "But how does it feel? Can you move it? Can you test it?" I convinced her to test it and she said, "It still hurts. But thank you. I'm sure it will get better," as if she was in a hurry to get the whole thing over with. I asked, "But how is the level of pain? Is it less?" She responded, "Yes, it is less."

I said, "OK, let's pray again." I prayed again and the pain was even less. But she said, "Oh, I've had this for so many years. I'm sure it will get better sometime." It was religious unbelief. I responded, "Listen, forget about that! It's normal for me to pray several times and the pain gets less until it's gone. This happens all the time, and I want you to leave here completely pain-free tonight. Just let me pray again."

I prayed two more times and she was pain-free. Then because it was dark and there was a part of the trail where she could get hurt or fall down the hill if she stepped wrong, I walked behind her and her son with my phone's flashlight so she could see.

## 4. Metaphors to Explain the Mechanics of God's Power

Even though she was pain-free after I prayed the fourth time, I don't think that what happened sunk in until a few minutes later when we were near the end of the trail. Her knee wasn't hurting! The old lady started to realize that Jesus had healed her. She became happy and started chattering joyfully. She said it was like God sent an angel to her that night. Her son was also grateful and they gave me a ride home. It was touching to see the old lady's happiness!

Here's the lesson: I didn't quit because she wasn't receptive at first! But I kept soaking her in God's goodness and striking again with God's word until she was healed. Maybe she seemed like a tough nut to crack, but she just needed a little soaking! God's love pursued her in spite of the religious unbelief and disappointment of the past.

There was a guy at the local drug and alcohol recovery house whose leg didn't have the proper circulation. Wounds were opening up, the flesh was starting to rot, he went around limping, and he had trouble sleeping at night because of the pain. So many other people were healed on several of my visits, but he was still suffering. One time they brought me into the dorm and he was laying there on the bed, moaning. I laid my hands on his leg and commanded it to be healed in Jesus' name, but he felt little or no difference.

Some people started questioning with human reasoning, but I responded and said, "God revealed his will in Jesus, and Jesus healed all who came to him. Scripture says now is the time of God's favor.[266] We've persevered before and seen people healed, and we're going to keep persevering for José and praying for him again, because it's not God's will for him to be suffering like this."

The next time I was there I said to them all, "Jesus deserves your healing, because he paid for it with his blood! It's not a matter of God deciding to heal you or not, but of God's Spirit being released through us. We are stubborn about seeing Jesus get what he deserves! God is glorified when people are healed. Some of you have received prayer before and still are having issues. Even if you've received prayer before, don't be discouraged, but come again so that we can glorify Jesus."

He received prayer again, and all the pain left! I was just talking to him on Saturday, about four months later. He was telling me how all the pus and open wounds had dried up. It was so wonderful to see him walking normally and without pain!

When we ministered and didn't see the change immediately, I didn't put the blame on him. Neither did I say in my heart, "It didn't work." I just kept soaking him with God's goodness and I told him, "It's not God's will for you to be suffering like this. We are going to keep persevering for you."

You are also like a sponge for God's presence. Immerse yourself and be saturated, so when you are squeezed, God's glory pours out! You overflow! I get so saturated and charged up with glory in my soul that I can't express it, but it pours out in tears. I go look for someone who is hurting, because I want to express the glory I feel in my heart.

Some people are missing what's most important when it comes to the many manifestations of God's Spirit. Many people want a how-to guide. However, you can only understand the things of God's Spirit by God's Spirit, so what's most important is walking in communion with God until you get so inundated with his Spirit that it overflows.

We teach some practical things about recognizing God's voice and acting in faith. But, when people ask, "How do you see?" it's hard to explain. How do you see what conditions people have before you even go to that place? How do you see their lives, or into their bodies? One of the best ways I can describe it is "love sees." When you're overflowing with God's love, you see into people and into their lives. All the manifestations of God's Spirit work as overflowing love expressed through faith.

# 4. Metaphors to Explain the Mechanics of God's Power

## *A Hammer*

The prophet Elisha told King Joash of Israel to shoot an arrow. Elisha proclaimed, "The Lord's arrow of victory over Aram!" Then he told the king to strike the ground with the arrows. The king, lacking in zeal, only struck the ground three times. Elisha was angry and said, "You should have struck five or six times. Then you would have struck down Aram until you had made an end of it, but now you will only strike down Aram three times."[267]

Similarly, God says in Jeremiah 23:29 that his word is like fire and like a hammer that breaks the rock. Fire has a continuous action. Likewise, you don't usually break up a big rock with only one blow of a hammer. You keep hitting it.

The "God is controlling everything" mentality thinks of miracles as simply being a matter of God doing it or deciding not to. People who think like that generally do not keep striking at the issue with God's word. They don't see much change, so they assume that God said "no" or it wasn't God's time and they stop striking at the issue. But scripture says we look not at things that are seen, but at things that are unseen![268]

People with that mentality can't understand how we pray and a person's sight improves but it's not yet perfect. They think, "God doesn't do things halfway." This is why it's important, when we minister healing, to evaluate the situation before we pray, then test it and pray again. We often use a scale of 1-10 for pain, with 10 being extreme pain and 1 being light pain. Did you pray and the pain went from a 9 to a 6? Keep striking until it's gone. Is the pain gone but the mobility still limited? Keep striking!

I have seen severe and constant pain from cancer leave completely as a person received ministry, but it ended up coming back and they died from cancer! It's not easy. That's why it takes courage and perseverance to keep growing in Jesus and obeying his command to heal the sick. It's why we need the Holy Spirit to strengthen our hearts. If I'd given up after those discouraging experiences, other people would not be free now!

People ask, "Why?" The story of Joash striking the arrows on the ground is a Biblical explanation. God isn't playing games with us and he's not wishy-washy. But spiritual dynamics are at work and we must remain firm and continue striking the enemy until he is completely destroyed. God's power coming on that person and driving out the pain was real.

Scripture says, "God sent his word and healed them."[269] God's word is in our mouths like a sword[270] and in our hands like a hammer to strike the work of the enemy. God's word is the means by which he heals people. Jesus, in his parable of the Sower, talked about some seed that was eaten by birds, scorched by the sun because the soil was shallow, or choked by weeds.[271]

This shows the need to guard and cultivate God's word in our hearts. Yet many people falsely assume "God said no" to what he has already said "Yes" about in his word. They allow the seed of God's word to be eaten, scorched, or choked out by adversity. When you pray for someone once and see no change, do you give up? Or do you guard God's word in your heart?

I have learned to keep striking until I see in my heart that Satan's work is totally destroyed! I don't want to be like King Joash, only experiencing a temporary victory.

Many miracles do happen instantly or almost instantly. How do you know if you need to keep striking? Look in the Spirit! How? You need God's help! The more you let the Holy Spirit flow through you, you grow in sensitivity to be able to see the invisible.

I spend a lot of time watching the meetings on YouTube with Mark Hemans and Jesus Encounter Ministries. Mark sometimes sees that something is done even when it doesn't yet look like it is naturally. He'll sometimes say, "You're free!" even when the demon is still manifesting. Later, people come back and testify that they are free. In other cases, he keeps releasing God's power, striking repeatedly at the

## 4. Metaphors to Explain the Mechanics of God's Power

problem until he senses or sees that the healing or deliverance is complete.

## *Fire*

God's word is also like fire. It continues to devour. It continues working. Think of a person who had chronic pain and didn't feel much difference at the moment they received ministry, but by the end of the day all the pain was gone. The person ministering set the problem on fire with God's word, and that fire kept burning until it was consumed.

Last night I went to pray for a man who was almost blind from complications of diabetes. When I got there, I felt God was prompting me to pray for his wife first, although nobody had mentioned any of her health issues. She was quickly healed of bad stomach pain caused by an infection. Then I said I saw God touching her head. We didn't know what the issue was, but she felt lots of heat on her head. I asked her about her neck, and God healed her of neck pain.

I felt that those quick miracles were to encourage her and her daughter so they would join me in praying for the husband. We all prayed. First his pancreas and belly got hot, and then his eyes also got hot. We tested his vision and he was able to see that I was holding up two fingers, but only from about 8 feet away. We kept praying and thanking God and tested his vision again. It wasn't much better, but God's power was still on him.

We prayed for quite a while longer and tested his vision again. Now he could easily see how many fingers I was holding up from an even longer distance, but his vision still needed to improve more.

I encouraged the family with some more testimonies and explained that God's word is like fire and continues burning. Thanking and praising God for what he is doing is like fanning the flames. I told them to keep thanking the Lord and send me an update in 24 hours. Before I left, I asked what he was feeling. He was still feeling God's fire burning in his belly and on his eyes as I left.

Last year I prayed for an older lady who'd suffered eight strokes. She walked with a limp because one side of her body was weaker than the other. I prayed for her with the family for about 20 minutes. Her head got hot and her strength was returning. Everyone felt the heat radiating off of her when they put their hands near her head.

We went on to pray for other family members, but she continued to feel the heat on her head. Two hours later when we left, she was still feeling God's fire burning on her head. And I didn't see her limping at all anymore when she walked!

Understanding that God's word keeps burning like fire will help you to persevere, stand firm, and not get discouraged. When you have improvement or change in a situation but you don't yet see 100% naturally, keep looking at what is unseen, not what is seen, and fan the flames by praising and thanking God for what he is doing!

Keep feeding the fire and fanning the flame! Don't throw a bucket of cold water on it by getting discouraged and falling into unbelief! God's word must be combined with faith to benefit those who hear it,[272] just as fire needs oxygen!

## *A Sword*

The sword of the Spirit is the Word of God.[273] Wielding that sword is your responsibility! Many religious people just say, "God is in control" and figure God will act if he wants to, instead of picking up their swords and using them. The sword of the Lord is in your hands![274]

Sometimes when I go pray for people, I feel like the wild Scottish warrior who goes into battle swinging a huge sword in circles. I get so consumed with God's word that I'm oblivious to whatever I see or don't see happening naturally. I just keep swinging the sword. Get carried away with God's word!

## 4. Metaphors to Explain the Mechanics of God's Power

I've been in many religious environments where the people are open to the miraculous but they think that healing is my spiritual gift. They don't understand that I am simply acting in the spiritual realm by swinging my sword, and they are not. Not one person among them speaks aggressively, "Pain, get out! Be healed in Jesus' name!" If they would use their swords, they would also get results.

Have you ever heard that words cut deeper than knives? Just as a person in the realm of darkness curses, we can bless people. Have you heard a long string of profanity come through the mouth of a person who is enraged? That is an evil spirit expressing itself through their mouth. Why don't we hear Christians blessing and speaking God's word with the same whole-hearted intensity so the Holy Spirit expresses himself through our mouths?

It's the same principle, just a different spirit. Many people in the realm of darkness act regularly in the spiritual realm to curse and destroy people, but few Christians know how to come out swinging and act in the spiritual realm to bless people and destroy what is hurting them! Instead, many Christians are still thinking of healing, deliverance, and miracles as mysterious superpowers that some Christians receive and others don't!

## *Rain And Snow*

Isaiah 55:10-11 (NIV) As the rain and the snow come down from heaven, and do not return to it without watering the earth and making it bud and flourish, so that it yields seed for the sower and bread for the eater, so is my word that goes out from my mouth: It will not return to me empty, but will accomplish what I desire and achieve the purpose for which I sent it.

The seeds sprouting and roots growing underground after a rainstorm are invisible. We don't see the effects immediately. It takes time for the earth to bud and flourish. Yet Christians often judge that God's word "didn't work" if they don't see immediate change.

Lightning's impact is sudden and immediately tangible. Each blow of a hammer or sword affects change. Fire burns until it devours. Rain causes plants to flourish, but we don't see them growing minute by minute. God's power may manifest in all of these different ways.

I took a friend to a rescue mission last Thursday. A few people rededicated their lives to Christ or received deliverance, and many were healed. One of the men had pain in his body and his hands shook violently. We prayed and the pain left, but his hands were still shaking. I chose to ignore that and thank the Holy Spirit for his work.

After praying for some other people and eating lunch, we saw the man again and his hands were normal! Yet we had prayed for another man who was shaking and didn't see the shaking stop.

My friend was trying to keep track of the testimonies. He remarked, "Two people were trembling. One was healed, but one wasn't."

I thought about what he said. Neither one stopped trembling immediately when we prayed. We saw one man again later and he was no longer trembling. The other, we didn't see again. Why assume that the other man was not healed? What if he also is no longer trembling and we just didn't see him again to confirm it?

Some people feel no manifestation or change when receiving ministry, but days or weeks later we find they were healed. I never pray for a person and say, "He wasn't healed" if I don't see a manifestation. I may say, "He didn't feel any difference at the moment."

I sometimes do make the mistake of assuming, "It didn't work," if I don't see a natural change, but I'm still learning and growing! As we grow in faith, we learn to doubt the doubts and not stress over how things appear. "How do you know he wasn't healed? I'm not so sure about that!"

## 4. Metaphors to Explain the Mechanics of God's Power

I overheard one of the recovery house leaders talking about his back pain. He'd already been healed of a foot injury, so I said, "Why didn't you tell me earlier? Let's pray now."

He'd been thrown by a horse when he was 12 years old, and had back pain ever since then. I prayed a few times. He felt no manifestation, change, or reduction in pain. I chose to keep believing that the Lord was working.

I saw him again months later and he told me, "Remember when you prayed for me? I didn't feel any difference. My back hurt just as much. Then 90 days later, I was lying on my sofa at home. I remembered how you prayed for me, and my back popped. I had that problem all my life since I was 12, and I've never had it again."

He spoke as if God had arbitrarily decided not to heal him when we first prayed, but instead to do it three months later. We know that isn't true. This man didn't understand the mechanics of miracles. God had sent his word and it was not going to return void. We just didn't see the lightning flash until three months later. His thoughts at that moment on the couch triggered heaven's supernatural manifestation. I can't explain exactly why he felt no change the first time, but I can tell you that spiritual dynamics are in play. God's power may be present and his word has gone forth, but there are "triggers" that cause the lightning to flash so we see the manifestation. Even thoughts often trigger the supernatural.

## *God's River*

Although the lightning metaphor is helpful, I'm not encouraging you to develop a theology of "I released everything I had so now I'm empty again!" Rather, God's desire is that the Holy Spirit flow through us as a river. It's an endless supply.

The prophet Ezekiel had a vision of water coming out from under the threshold of God's temple. The further he went, the deeper the water became. After a thousand cubits, the water was ankle deep. Another thousand, and it was knee-deep.

## The Mechanics of Miracles

Another thousand, and it was waist-deep. After another thousand cubits, it was a river that nobody could cross!

The river goes on to enter the Dead Sea, making the salty water fresh. Swarms of living creatures live wherever the river flows, with large numbers of fish. Where the river flows, everything lives! Fruit trees grow on each bank of the river, with their fruit for food and their leaves for healing! But the swamps and marshes will not be made fresh.[275]

In the New Covenant, we are the temple![276] God's river flows from us! Jesus said that rivers of living water would flow from the innermost being of whoever believes in him![277]

The river flows out of us, not in! Many Christians are turned inward, focused constantly on receiving something from God rather than on giving his life and riches to the world. Much of what you will receive from God is by giving! Let God's river flow outward and it will supply your need as well as the needs of those you are ministering to.

When I started ministering healing, I often tried ministering healing to myself without experiencing any results. Yet I have repeatedly been healed myself as I minister to others. The river of God flowing through me to other people destroyed the infection attacking my own body! Once after injuring my elbow, I prayed for myself and it still hurt. Later, as I was praying for other people, I felt a heat come on my elbow. At first, I thought it was another word of knowledge, but then I realized I had just been healed as God's river flowed through me.

The river keeps getting deeper as you continue in it. Did you pray for someone, persevere, and see no change? Did you feel discouraged? The best response, in my experience, has often been to keep praying for as many people as you can, and then come back to that person again! Don't let it bother you! Don't get caught up asking, "Why?" Just keep going in God's river and the manifestation of his glory will increase! I've often seen people healed by doing this when we didn't see change the first time, or the first few times.

## 4. Metaphors to Explain the Mechanics of God's Power

At the beginning of God's river, the thirsty are refreshed and cool their feet. It keeps getting deeper until even people who are resistant have power encounters with God and get swept away in his river! In one moment, a person is a mocking persecutor, and a minute later they are weeping and wailing or rolling on the ground and praising God in tongues!

Instead of the mentality of begging God to send revival (as if you wanted it more than he does), understand that as you keep going in God's river, it gets deeper. Remember that it must flow out of you! Many Christians live as swamps or marshes, with little flowing out, and the swamps and marshes will not be made fresh!

Last Saturday we saw God pouring out his heavenly river at a women's drug and alcohol recovery house. Many asked for prayer because they had seen the miracles Jesus did on our previous visits. One wanted to be healed of epilepsy. Another lady was asking for prayer for something as well, but I said, "First, I want you to pray for this lady with epilepsy."

She said, "Me! No way!" That reaction is common. Some people think I can pray because I have some more merit than they do. I try to get them to see that it's not true. I was just as desperate and in need of a Savior as every person in that recovery house! Jesus rescued me! I responded, "Why not you? It's not about who prays, but it is about the name of Jesus!"

She went and got another lady to pray. I said, "She can pray too, but I want you to lay your hand on her head and pray." She finally did, repeating after me, "Be healed in Jesus' name. Epilepsy, go!"

She was overwhelmed and had tears in her eyes as she tangibly felt God's power flowing through her into the epileptic woman. Later, I found out that she received the answer to her own prayer request as she prayed for the other lady. She had wanted prayer for anxiety. As God's river flowed through her into the other lady, she felt her body get light and the burden lift!

I do this as much as possible. I grab other Christians who feel totally inadequate and have them lay their hands on the person. The miracles happen through them so that they know it's not about who prays, but it is about the name of Jesus and us acting as the body of Christ! We are not adequate. Jesus is!

For God's river to flow out from you, you're going to have to get your focus off yourself and your own problems, walk in communion with God, and speak and act in faith! Don't wait for God to send revival! Be revival now!

In times of ministering healing, Randy Clark asks people to wave both hands in the air if they are 80% or more better. He asks them to wave one hand if they felt improvement or felt a manifestation of God's power, even if it isn't 80% better yet. He then has them receive ministry again, and it is often 100% the next time!

Someone who doesn't understand the mechanics of miracles asks, "Why would they only feel less pain? Shouldn't there be no pain if God really healed them? Why would God do it halfway?" But it happens by God's river flowing through us. We look for what God is doing, and thank him for it. We look for improvement, and as we keep going in God's river, it gets deeper!

Maybe you're used to water up to the waist. This challenge to enter the new normal God has for you isn't just for those who have never ministered in God's power. It's also for those who are ministering in power but allowing your faith to be limited by your previous experience. There is a flow of the river that nobody can swim in. There's a manifestation of God's glory that challenges the mocker and unbeliever! Keep going on in God! There are no limits on his part!

# 5. Jesus Was Crucified and Rose Again

## *Jesus' Torn Body Is Our Open Heaven*

Many truths may help Christians to walk in power, but two specific truths are foundational. The first is that God is an invisible Spirit but is seen when manifest in flesh, so Jesus came in the flesh and fully revealed God's will and nature. The second is that the heavens are open!

Hebrews chapters 9 and 10 teach that the holiest place which Jesus entered was heaven itself,[278] and the veil that was torn was his body! It admonishes us to enter the holiest place, heaven itself, through the torn body of Jesus.[279] The heavens were torn open when Jesus' body was torn, giving us full access to God, which is access to heaven now! We can approach the Father with confidence, cleansed by Jesus' blood from all unrighteousness, having the same boldness with which Jesus himself approaches God the Father! Jesus is not ashamed to call us his siblings![280]

Christians accept as good doctrine that we have full access to God's presence through Jesus Christ, but often act and speak as if this weren't true. The truth doesn't benefit them because they are double-minded about it, so they lack experience of God's power and glory. Then they think they need something more or something new!

I had a vision in which God showed me one of the main causes of powerlessness in the Church. Many people were praying and fasting and banging their fists on a big wall, crying out, "Oh God, that you would rend the heavens and come down!"[281] With great effort they were endlessly begging and pleading for God to open the heavens, send revival, come with a mighty visitation, and give them authority over the works of the enemy.

Some were using a tree trunk as a battering ram to try to break through the wall. They were frustrated, but figured that maybe they just needed to try harder!

Right beside them was an open door! They seemed blind to the door which they could simply walk through. They didn't need to break through the wall! Only a few people saw the door. They were walking in and out easily, full of joy, with radiant faces and miracles happening all around them.

They prayed continually,[282] and their prayers were answered quickly, before they could even close their mouths from forming the words.[283] They were constantly praying because they knew they had what they asked of the Father. They exercised dominion over sickness and the works of the enemy.

I understood that God's power is in the gospel,[284] yet many give mental assent to the gospel, but fail to embrace it experientially. Such Christians pray as if Jesus had never died for their sins, risen from the dead, or come in the flesh. I had been in that group for many years of frustration and powerlessness! But now I was living a life of miracles, walking in freely through the door (Jesus' torn body), constantly overwhelmed by God's goodness, and often on the verge of tears throughout the week as I saw the mighty works of Jesus.

To plead with God for open heavens is to pray as if Jesus never died to make the way for us to approach the Father. To plead with him to give us authority over the works of the enemy is to deny identification with the resurrection of Jesus, by which we have been seated in heavenly places far above all power and authority![285] To ask God to come down is to deny that Jesus has come in the flesh and God is with us![286]

That kind of prayer is one of the primary causes of powerlessness in the church. What most of the church thinks is normal is pitiful, and what should be normal is thought of as

## 5. Jesus Was Crucified and Rose Again!

extraordinary! God's power is in the gospel, and lack of power shows that we don't believe the gospel! We may give mental assent to good theology, but we are acting as if it isn't true!

## *There Is Only One Door*

Jesus' redemptive work is sufficient for every area of your life! He said, "I am the gate"[287] and, "nobody comes to the Father except through me."[288] All of God's promises are "yes and amen" in Christ![289]

We are saved by God's power through faith, not of works or of ourselves but as the gift of God, so that no man can boast.[290] Salvation as taught in scripture is Heaven's dominion in every area of your life, and it's by grace the whole way. It includes healing, peace, provision, and deliverance. As you received Jesus, continue living in him.[291]

Whenever we try to attain by some other means that which God has freely given us in Christ, we cut ourselves off from the flow of God's grace![292] God's grace is power. To walk in God's power, you must freely receive his grace!

A few years ago, I heard the Lord shout, "Come to me with empty hands!" I fell back in my seat because of the glory of his voice. Then the Holy Spirit showed me that the statement "Nobody shall approach me empty-handed"[293] was said on Mount Sinai in Arabia, which Galatians says corresponds to Hagar who is in slavery with her children, but we are children of the free woman under the better covenant![294] The gospel is, "Come, all you who have no money! Come, buy and eat, without money and without cost!"[295]

God resists the proud but gives grace to the humble,[296] so come to God in humility with empty hands and he will fill you to overflowing! But if you come to God with pride presenting your own works before him, you will go away empty-handed![297]

Much of the Church today has fallen into a great error in which they talk more about our offerings than about Jesus Christ and his redemptive work on our behalf! They preach that we must receive God's blessing through our tithes and offerings. Then if anything good happens, people testify about what they put in the offering instead of talking about what Jesus did for them.

Many preachers talk about so many "keys to breakthrough" that everyone nearly forgets that the key is Jesus and his redemptive work on our behalf. What if your real hindrance is all your "keys" and "principles" that are seducing you away from the simplicity that is in Christ?[298]

If you didn't first get saved by what you put in the offering, don't try to continue in your salvation by it.[299] Which sacrifice do you think God is more impressed with? What you threw in the offering plate, or the blood of Jesus Christ?

The punishment of our peace was upon Jesus.[300] The word "peace"[301] in the Old Testament is synonymous with the word "sozo"[302] for salvation in Greek. "Peace" in scripture is a practical word, applying to every area of our lives. If experiencing God's peace and redemption in any area of our lives depended on tithes or offerings, it would mean that Jesus' sacrifice alone was not sufficient for full redemption! So cut out the religiosity and honour Jesus and the price he paid!

If all of God's promises are "yes and amen" in Jesus,[303] then they do not depend on tithes or offerings. As long as you attempt to attain by any other means that which Jesus has accomplished for you by his death and resurrection, you will remain blind to the riches you have in Christ. Giving and generosity are an overflow of the abundant grace[304] that we have in Jesus Christ, just as healing and prophecy are. Giving money must never be presented as a means of attaining God's grace!

The good news that Jesus preached to the poor[305] was not, "Give me a tenth of your money and generous offerings on top of that, and you'll be blessed!" Neither did the apostles say, "Give me a bigger offering this time and you'll get your breakthrough." Rather, they taught we have every spiritual blessing in Jesus Christ![306]

## 5. Jesus Was Crucified and Rose Again!

One major cause of powerlessness is listening to teachers who suggest that what you put in the offering connects you to God. Then you no longer relate to God through Christ alone. That stops the flow of the river of life and cuts off your connection of communion with God.

Have you ever experienced that? The preacher said, "I want you to sow a seed like you've never sown before for your breakthrough." Then, when your breakthrough doesn't come, you think you must not have put enough money in the offering. The next meeting is another version of the same message. If you still need to "sow" more this week to get blessed, obviously, whatever you sowed the last time wasn't sufficient. Whatever you give is never enough!

Every such message tells you that you lack, promoting unbelief concerning what Jesus has accomplished. If you listen to such preachers, you never simply receive the fullness of blessing[307] in Jesus through what Jesus has done.

Why would your motivation for giving be getting a "breakthrough" if you believe that Jesus accomplished all and is completely victorious on your behalf? Why would your motivation be gaining a blessing that you lack if you believe you've been given every spiritual blessing in Jesus[308] and all you need for life and godliness is found in the knowledge of Christ?[309]

The apostle Paul taught that if the inheritance comes by law, grace and faith are annulled and the promise is cancelled![310] Many in the church live a life of spiritual poverty because they have cancelled God's promises for them by trying to attain the inheritance by the law rather than by grace through faith. A life lived by God's grace manifests in spiritual riches.

Many moves that have started in the Spirit with revival, glory, and miracles have lost the glory in that way. The focus moves further and further away from Jesus Christ and his redemptive work, and soon the miracles are stories from the past. I've seen God's glory manifesting in a meeting, but then as they took the offering, I saw putrid black smoke! Don't start in the Spirit and end in the flesh![311]

## The Mechanics of Miracles

The biggest church in my city started with a great move of the Holy Spirit. Randy Clark and Global Awakening visited their congregation years ago and they experienced healings and miracles. Sadly, like so many other groups, they started in the Spirit and ended in the flesh. They have now lost much of the power and glory, and fallen into heresy.

Their pastor preached, "If you want to be a part of my ministry and receive my anointing, you must eat my flesh and drink my blood." It's no longer Jesus' ministry. It's no longer Jesus' anointing. Jesus' flesh and blood is no longer central. The connection and loyalty to their group and pastor has replaced the people's connection and loyalty to Jesus. They say, "Sow a big seed and you'll be blessed." But that's actually how they lost the glory!

You can only have mixture for so long. This scenario has been repeated innumerable times. A group started in the Spirit, but the focus turned away from the centrality of Jesus and his redemptive work. The leaven of legalism entered.[312] Even if there were still some healings and miracles, there was no longer the same glory. If the church doesn't get rid of the leaven,[313] it eventually works through the whole batch[314] and the miracles and the Holy Spirit's move become only a story from the past.

God is putting his finger on this in the Church. A pure gospel manifests God's power. Do you want a message that is confirmed with power? Do you want unbelievers to physically feel God's glory in the atmosphere as you speak? It has to be a pure gospel message, and it has to be free, without leaven.

I've had hundreds of experiences with God's glory manifesting in a physical way, and I've learned what caused or triggered those tangible manifestations. God's glory manifests through the simple message about Jesus and what he has done for us, with no mixture.

## 5. Jesus Was Crucified and Rose Again!

## *Jesus, the Seed God Sowed*

If I preach and I see the people manipulated to give out of guilt or in an attempt to get a miracle, I won't accept the offering. When attending a meeting, if the person taking the offering tells people they will get their breakthrough by sowing a seed, I refuse to participate in their sin by giving in the offering. To give in that offering would be like participating in a pagan sacrifice.

I honour Jesus and all he has accomplished for me. Those receiving an offering often claim that by giving in it, we can obtain blessings and breakthroughs which Jesus has already attained for us by his redemptive work. Giving in such an offering with that motivation is an act of unbelief regarding what Jesus has done for us. To contribute to such an offering is to dishonour Jesus Christ, belittling his death on the cross and his resurrection on our behalf.

The mark of every false religion is that people seek salvation by works. They approach their god (or gods) by some way other than through Jesus in order to gain the deity's blessing or avoid its curse.

"Antichrist" means not only, "against Christ" but also, "in place of Christ." Since "Christ" means "Anointed One," we also understand that the antichrist spirit offers something else in place of the anointing. It puts something else in the place of Christ's redemptive work.

I live in a city of almost 3 million people and full of churches. Many of them have fallen into another gospel that is no gospel at all.[315] Any unbiased observer can see that they talk more about the offering than about Jesus Christ! They have lots of hype, but power is lacking! It's empty!

Week after week, church leaders tell the congregations that the key to their blessing is sowing another seed. Yet we experience more of God's glory manifest in power in one day of walking in God's grace than we could sitting in their meetings all year! I refuse to participate in their sin by giving to such preachers! They don't have a single pastor or member in their churches who is experiencing the glory that I know! Why? It's not by my own merit or godliness![316] I come to God with empty hands and receive his grace!

I have sat in too many meetings and heard that the way to get God's blessing is sowing a bigger seed, yet I didn't see anyone in the meeting blessed as much as the homeless guy I prayed for the night before who was healed and struck mute in God's glory. He didn't give me a cent! I am reaping a harvest from the greatest Seed ever sown, Jesus Christ,[317] who died and was buried as a seed in the ground and now has resurrected and is bearing much fruit!

Two years ago, I visited a meeting with lots of hype after what seemed to be an hour of talking about getting God's blessing by sowing your best seed. They said, "people are going to get out of wheelchairs in this church." Yet someone was there in a wheelchair and I didn't see anyone else laying hands on him!

It was only a few weeks later that a guy stood up from his wheelchair and walked without pain at the bus stop in front of that church. It wasn't because of a seed he sowed! Learn the difference between hype and the anointing! The anointing comes and God's glory manifests through a pure and powerful gospel message that glorifies Jesus and doesn't put anything in his place!

Many have been sitting in their services and putting money in the offering for years but still feel inadequate to even pray for someone! They are in a religious system that has replaced Jesus' redemptive work with their offering. Because of this, they aren't even in communion with God!

Meanwhile, I go late at night to a burger joint and explain to a young Christian the simple, glorious truth about what Jesus has done for us. When he understands, he starts seeing Jesus do miracles through his hands right away!

Many churches in this city are constantly manipulating people to give with carrot-and-stick guilt trips and hours spent preaching on tithes and offerings. They have millions in

## 5. Jesus Was Crucified and Rose Again!

revenue. They see the people as assets for their ministries who are there to serve them.

Yet drug and alcohol recovery houses and ministries caring for the orphan and elderly are neglected. It is easy for a large church to spend more in one night on an offering for a famous guest preacher with lots of hype and mere human wisdom but little power, than they will give to care for the needy in a year.

I recently found that in some of the recovery houses almost nobody even had a Bible. Some people don't even have a pair of flip-flops. It is easy for a single person to do more to support one of these recovery houses than what any of those entire churches are doing! We give at recovery houses as the outflow of having already received God's grace in Christ, and not as a means of attaining it.

God's glory manifests when we become servants of all,[318] especially of the least,[319] for the sake of Jesus. We see heaven's riches poured out with wonderful manifestations of God's glory, including deaf ears opened, sight restored, and surgeries cancelled!

When I go to those recovery houses and poor neighbourhoods with dirt roads, I sometimes feel I'm in heaven! None of them give me a "seed" or an offering. Heaven is poured out on them in glory and miracles in a way that most church members who throw their "seed" into the offering every week to be blessed could hardly imagine!

If they really get more of God's blessing and grace based on how much money they throw in the offering, I would like to see in their meetings the same miracles I regularly see among poor and broken people who give me nothing. God sends the rich away empty, but fills the hungry with good things![320] The proud come to God with their own works rather than approaching him in humility with empty hands. The poor and broken receive the abundance that's always just out of reach for those who are trying to bargain with God and don't know they have nothing to offer!

## Jesus' Death Means I Have Died

Those who are in Jesus Christ have died with him and also resurrected with him in newness of life.[321] Therefore we must consider ourselves dead to sin and alive to righteousness.[322]

Many Christians regularly remark, "We're just sinners," but they are doing the opposite of what Paul taught us in Romans 6. They are considering themselves alive to sin and dead to righteousness! Since they believe that they are still sinners, they have an expectation that Christians will always fail. I believe that is a major reason why such groups often have so much sexual immorality among them.

All have sinned and fallen short of God's glory,[323] but the one who trusts in Jesus considers it to be a fact that "the old sinner I used to be has died with Jesus, and I have now been resurrected with Jesus in newness of life." Whoever is in Christ is a new creation! Old things have passed away and all things have become new![324] Colossians chapter 3 teaches us that we put off the deeds of the flesh because we consider it to be a fact that we have already died to sin with Christ![325]

The New Testament repeatedly calls us saints.[326] A saint is the opposite of a sinner! We receive God's free gift of righteousness[327] when we consider it a fact that we have died with Jesus and been resurrected with Jesus. Yielding to the free gift of righteousness produces the fruit of holiness.[328]

We were darkness, but now we are light in Jesus![329] Darkness cannot have fellowship with light,[330] and God is light.[331] The free gift of righteousness through faith and identification with Jesus' death and resurrection makes us light so that we can have communion with God.

As we talked about in the last chapter, our hearts are like clouds or capacitors, and they are charged as we walk in communion with God. Many Christians have no communion with God because of guilt and condemnation! Because we have been made light by God's grace, we walk as children of light[332] and experience communion with God.

## 5. Jesus Was Crucified and Rose Again!

The mindset that we are still sinners and will live a life of failure is deeply rooted in an erroneous Gnostic understanding of how scripture uses the term "the flesh." It interprets Romans 7 in a way that contradicts the previous chapter and the following chapter!

The Gnostics denied Jesus came in the flesh because they believed the physical realm was base and corrupt, and only the spiritual was holy. Do you ever hear Christians say, "We will always sin because we are human?" That is exactly the thinking behind the Gnostic's denial that Jesus came as God in a human body! Jesus' incarnation shows us that the body is holy!

A detailed study shows that the New Testament often uses the term "the flesh" to talk about living by the law and mere human ability as the Galatians did.[333] They trusted in being "circumcised in the flesh."[334] Paul's description of living in the flesh in Romans chapter seven speaks of living by the law and trying to please God by human effort. He did not say, "We will always sin because we are human!"

Immediately following chapter seven, Romans 8:9 says that we are not in the flesh, but in the Spirit, if God's Spirit lives in us. You are not even saved if Christ's Spirit doesn't live in you.[335] Therefore, if you are in Christ, you are not in the flesh.

When Paul wrote that those who are indwelt by the Holy Spirit are not in the flesh, he didn't mean, "You no longer are in a human body." He was saying, as he did in Galatians, that we are no longer under the law and living by mere human effort if we are in Christ. Rather, we live by the Holy Spirit's empowerment.

I have often been with Christian groups and they soon see what happens in my life and say, "Jonathan has a spiritual gift." I want to scream, "Guys, you don't get it! This is what should be normal!" The truth is that nearly all of them are still calling themselves sinners because of their gnostic view of the term "the flesh," and that is hindering them from having communion with God! They don't have boldness and confidence to approach God the Father[336] through Jesus Christ.

Moses beheld God's glory, so his face radiated light.[337] However, the glory of the Old Covenant pales in comparison to the glory of the New Covenant which we have access to in Jesus![338] Stephen's face shone like that of an angel in the New Covenant![339] The way is open, so what is stopping us from walking in communion with God until our faces shine like those of angels?

Jesus is not ashamed to call us brothers.[340] If we understand this and trust in what Jesus has done for us, we know that we have full access to approach the throne of God the Father with the same confidence as Jesus himself has![341] If we are going to have communion with God who is light, we must understand that by grace and the free gift of righteousness, God has also made us light: saints, not sinners! Consider it to be a fact, and so walk in it!

It's wonderful to live with a clean conscience and in continual communion with God! If you stumble, quickly repent, receive God's grace, and get back to that place of communion! When I walk in such communion with God, I feel like I'm on the verge of tears all the time, filled with joy, with currents of God's love flowing through me!

## *Jesus' Death Broke Satan's Power and Freed Us from the Law of Sin and Death*

Jesus broke Satan's power by his death.[342] Jesus totally defeated Satan and made a mockery of him. Jesus disarmed the powers and authorities and made a spectacle of his victory over them.[343] The old law in letter, with its commandments and regulations that were against us, was nailed to the cross.[344]

Paul taught the Romans that they had been married to the old law, but by death they are freed from that law to belong to another.[345] We are not lawless, but we are under another law, the law of the Spirit of life in Christ.[346] This law produces life through grace and justification rather than producing death through condemnation. It empowers us and makes us partakers in God's nature.

### 5. Jesus Was Crucified and Rose Again!

Rather than trying to measure up by human efforts in order to have communion with God, the law of the Spirit of life puts us in communion with God by grace. His power and nature manifest through us by his own Spirit living in us!

We died with Jesus and were raised with him. We died to the old law and to our mere human efforts, and have been raised by God's power so as to live by the Holy Spirit's empowerment.

If we return to the Old Covenant we died to, attempting to live by the flesh and mere human effort, we've broken our identification with the death and resurrection of Jesus. The book of Galatians and many other New Testament passages that rebuke the Judaizers deal with that error. Yet, much of the church today still falls into the same error.

If you are living by the law of the Spirit of life, the fruit is righteousness, joy, and peace.[347] If you are living by the old law, you'll always be frustrated and the deeds of the flesh will be evident.

The power is not in mental assent to good doctrine, but in identifying with Jesus' death and resurrection. We understand what these truths mean for us and act accordingly.

If we try to break Satan's power or treat him as an armed enemy, we deny what Jesus accomplished by his death! The battle we fight is proclaiming Jesus' victory versus the lies of the enemy. When we go out to minister in power, we aren't trying to break Satan's power! Rather, we declare Jesus' victory and Satan's defeat accomplished on the cross!

## *Our Resurrection with Jesus Seats Us with Him in Heavenly Places*

We've been raised with Christ and seated with him in heavenly places, far above all power and authority. We who are in Christ have died to being "mere humans"[348] and have resurrected as heavenly people. Since we've died with Christ, we set our minds on things above and not on earthly things.[349] We put off the deeds of the flesh.[350]

# The Mechanics of Miracles

We have died with Christ to the earthly-minded, mere human way of thinking, so we put it off. We live by heavenly wisdom which seems foolish according to human wisdom, but the foolishness of God is wiser than human wisdom![351]

There is only one level of authority in Jesus, and it is seated with Christ, far above all power and authority.[352] Jesus gave his disciples authority to cast out demons and heal every sickness and disease.[353] But we are only able to walk in that authority as we live in identification with Jesus. His death was my death! His life is my life! Now I no longer live, but Jesus lives in me![354] The walk of power is giving up your life completely to Jesus and letting his Spirit manifest through you.

Being raised with Christ gives us access to the riches of heaven. If you understand that, it produces unspeakable joy.[355] Sometimes I feel like I am about to explode. I'm rich! I need to give it away! When you see someone hurting, you know you have what they need, because you have Jesus and all the riches that are in him! You are no longer preoccupied with your own needs, but with giving away the abundance you have to the world. "The Lord is my Shepherd. I shall not want!"[356]

When you understand heavenly riches, you see a mind destroyed by drugs and think, "I have what he needs! I have Jesus! His mind can be restored!" When you see a blind woman, you think, "I need to give her Jesus! She can see again! How can I not give away what I have! How can I leave her like that?" That's how heavenly-minded people think.

When you understand how rich you are in Jesus because of what his resurrection has accomplished for you, you'll be so bold that others will be shocked. Jesus was crucified for our sins and raised for our justification.[357] Most people sitting in church don't really believe that, and that's why so many ask, "Who am I to pray for someone? You pray for them." That is what keeps the church bound in powerlessness. The just are as bold as a lion.[358] Jesus' resurrection makes you bold!

You may have been the most timid person, but God's love gripping your heart will make you bold like a lion. It seems like withholding abundant food from a starving person if you

## 5. Jesus Was Crucified and Rose Again!

don't go up and give hurting people what you have. You'll hunt people down to give them Jesus. God's mercy is pursuing them. I have Jesus, so I have everything!

## *Jesus' Death Reveals God's Love*

What love is this, that our Savior died to rescue us when we were still sinners! God reveals his love through the death of his Son.[359] I remember sobbing as a child when I understood how Jesus suffered and died for me. I remember how thankful I was that he rescued me!

We don't just start the Christian life by understanding Jesus' death and resurrection and then go on to greater things. Rather, we continually remind ourselves of Jesus' death and resurrection and we live by these truths. We take communion to remind ourselves of Jesus' death and drink of God's love once again. Love is not found in us loving God first, but in his loving us.[360] First we receive, and then we love because he first loved us.[361] We drink of God's love, so it flows through us.

I was desperate, lost, helpless, and Jesus rescued me! Sometimes, I remember that and I see all the riches God has given me in Jesus, and I just start sobbing again. That is the place of humility, and God gives grace to the humble.[362] Sometimes, I come back from the recovery house and start sobbing because of God's love for the people there. When my heart is in that place, all of heaven flows through me!

I was recently at a ladies' recovery house and God brought my heart back to the time when I was 13 and thought I'd committed the unforgivable sin, but God's love came over me. The Holy Spirit said, "I not only forgive you, but I will do miracles through you." I wept as I remembered this during the worship time, knowing I deserved nothing but Jesus gave me everything.

Then came the time to minister. I stood up to speak, knowing I needed God's grace just as much as every lady there, and God had poured out his kindness to me in Christ. Heaven's river poured out and we saw one miracle after another. Many received deliverance from anxiety. Near the end, I asked if there was still anybody else who needed healing. A lady stood up and said, "I need healing from depression." As she came up to receive prayer, a demon began manifesting. I cried out, "Thank you Jesus!" She fell the ground, the spirit left with a scream, and all the other ladies stood up and applauded. We couldn't find a single woman who still had pain in her body by the end of the night.

That was high-level! The leader of our missions group once said, "That guy Jon: he's on another level!" The Holy Spirit spoke to me, "The highest level is the lowest place!" I was a sinner, and I've been saved by grace.

Thanksgiving is humility. Jesus told his disciples to rejoice not that the demons submitted, but that their names were written in the book of life.[363] When we thank God for saving us, it keeps us in the place of humility. When we lose that attitude of thanksgiving to Jesus for saving us, we lose humility and lose the flow of heaven.

Love is a key for walking in God's power. It keeps us going and makes our hearts burn with fervency. Love makes us aggressive and tenacious. It makes us persevere. However, it is possible for someone to exercise faith but have wrong motives and be lacking in love. The person who receives the manifestation of God's Spirit (such as healing or prophecy) benefits, but the one ministering doesn't benefit if they don't act in love.

We don't choose between power and love. They must go together! God's nature of love is manifest through his power! God's love motivates us to step out in faith and power.

## *Go Against the Flow if You're Not Happy with the Religious Status-Quo*

If you are happy with the religious status-quo, keep acting and thinking the same way as everyone else around you! However, if you want to experience something new and greater in God

## 5. Jesus Was Crucified and Rose Again!

than you have before, you'll probably have to go against the grain!

If you want to freely receive abundance of grace from heaven, then never give in an offering as a means of obtaining God's grace. Don't give when they take the offering that way. Only give as the outflow of God's grace that you have freely received in Jesus Christ! If you can't find a church in which you can give in that way, you may have to be creative about how to stay in Christian fellowship! There are home meetings, online meetings, street meetings, and many other ways to get together as the body of Christ. You can start your own church!

Encouraging you to give only as the outflow of God's grace angers many church leaders. But what is the fruit of their teaching? I don't see in their lives what feeds my hunger. If they are right about the way people must give, where are the Bibles and flip-flops for the people in the local recovery houses? Where is the peace, joy, and freedom? Why are so many people in their congregations, including leaders, struggling with porn? Where are the heavenly riches?

I recently was sharing with a men's group about the abundance of grace in Jesus Christ. A young man started freaking out and came up in the middle of the message saying, "You need to pray for me!" He later explained, "I've been Catholic all my life and I don't know who this guy is, but I never felt anything before like I did when he was talking. Then, I saw fire and smoke coming out of his body! I need to convert to being an Evangelical!" We explained that it's not about joining a specific group, but it is about knowing Jesus Christ and what Jesus has done for us.

What message comes with the manifestation of God's glory, confirmed with signs? We don't preach ourselves, but we preach Jesus![364] I told him that I'm just a disciple of Jesus Christ and he can be too, because what I'm sharing is for all who believe.

When that pure message is preached demons leave, people are healed, God's glory manifests tangibly, and unbelievers see signs. I don't see the same power and glory manifest when they say, "Give your best seed today and God will bless you 100-

fold!" I already have every spiritual blessing as I'm seated with Christ in heavenly places.[365] I have abundance, more than enough, lacking nothing in Christ! I'm complete in Jesus![366]

Many of the people who push back at what I'm saying about the flesh are struggling with pornography. Pastors are preaching, "We're all sinners and we're all going to fail," and they are on their third wife. I'm not saying this without mercy or in a spirit of accusation. But look at what their thinking is producing!

I'm not a strong Christian. I often feel I'm a weak Christian. I often have not been as steadfast and consistent in my walk with the Lord as I want to be. But God's power is at work in me by grace, and it's evident. I got to the point of giving up and saying, "I'm so tired of the cycles of sin and death in my life. Holy Spirit, I yield my life to you. Do what I can't. Jesus, I give you all my heart and soul." I let the free gift of righteousness produce the fruit of righteousness in me. I've seen Jesus, and I'm not satisfied with less!

By God's grace, I still have the same wife and I haven't looked at porn since I was 12 years old. Not because I've been a strong Christian, but because of the love and grace I've found in Jesus. God's power flowing through me has changed my desires.

The key to walking in God's power and miracles is the same as the key to freedom from addictions and besetting sins. It's the flow of God's River of life through the free gift of righteousness. The moment you try to connect to God through your offering or something else, you cut that flow.

The same flow heals the sick, casts out demons, and brings heaven's peace and joy into people's lives and relationships! It causes Jesus to be seen through your life! There are many manifestations but one Spirit and one flow of the river of heaven!

I'm shooting straight with humility and brokenness because I know what the message I'm sharing has produced in my life! I see many young Christians who are so hungry, and I want to help them. I feel compassion when I see them being

## 5. Jesus Was Crucified and Rose Again!

misguided to end up in the flesh when they had started in the Spirit!

# 6. The Heart

## *God's Garden*

"Paradise" means "God's garden."[367] God gave mankind a garden called Eden to cultivate.[368] Mankind lost Eden when the first Adam sinned,[369] but the second Adam,[370] Jesus, restores us to God's garden and full access to God's presence.[371] Those who are always experiencing great things in God have cultivated a heavenly reality in the gardens of their hearts.

<u>Proverbs 4:23 (AMPC)</u> Keep and guard your heart with all vigilance and above all that you guard, for out of it flow the springs of life.

Your heart is God's garden. Hebrews teaches that the holiest place in the true temple is heaven itself,[372] and we are the temple of God![373] He abides in man![374] Heaven's reality is the reality of God's presence,[375] and your heart is the inner sanctuary where you commune with God. If you commune with God, heaven is in your heart.

Tending that garden is your responsibility. Will you plant and water the seed of God's word?[376] Will you pull up the weeds? God's river flows from the temple,[377] which is within you, just as rivers flowed out of the Garden of Eden.[378] To walk in the new normal that God has for the church, your heart reality needs to be transformed.

Plant God's word in your heart by reading and meditating on scripture. Rip up the weeds by aggressively confronting lies and beliefs that are contrary to God's Word. Refuse to consider or meditate on that which is destructive. Be ruthless in confronting unbelief! Sow in prayer! Just as it takes persistence to lose weight or get in shape, tending the garden of your heart takes patience and perseverance. You will reap a tremendous harvest if you don't give up.[379]

Be deliberate and disciplined about praising and thanking the Lord in every circumstance.[380] Set your heart on heavenly things, not on earthly things.[381] Don't watch junk on TV, but instead, fill your heart with life. Keep going over testimonies.[382] Remind yourself of what God has done in your life and what you have seen him do for others.[383] Write it down!

Philippians 4:4-9 (NIV) Rejoice in the Lord always. I will say it again: Rejoice! Let your gentleness be evident to all. The Lord is near. Do not be anxious about anything, but in every situation, by prayer and petition, with thanksgiving, present your requests to God. And the peace of God, which transcends all understanding, will guard your hearts and your minds in Christ Jesus.

Finally, brothers and sisters, whatever is true, whatever is noble, whatever is right, whatever is pure, whatever is lovely, whatever is admirable—if anything is excellent or praiseworthy—think about such things. Whatever you have learned or received or heard from me, or seen in me—put it into practice. And the God of peace will be with you.

## *The Weed of Disappointment*

I recently visited a recovery house to bring Bibles and prayed for a lady who was totally deaf in one ear and partially blind in one eye. The other eye also had poor vision. Her ear opened quickly so that when I snapped my fingers in each ear, she heard the same volume in both! She could now see to read what she was previously unable to read from that distance. I prayed again and she read another sign with smaller letters, saying, "I

## 6. The Heart

never knew what that sign said before because I was never able to read it!"

Then I remembered that I had prayed for her before and didn't see anything change. What if I had let disappointment grow like a weed in my heart, with human reasoning trying to figure everything out and asking, "Why didn't it work before?" What if I had been looking at things seen and not things unseen?

If you tend the garden of your heart, you won't allow those weeds to grow and you won't even consider the situation from a merely human viewpoint. There have been times in which I ministered to someone who needed healing, but there was no apparent change, and I felt disappointment coming on. Yet various times, when I rejected that disappointment and refused to give it a place in my heart, God's power remained on them and I later found they were healed.

A few years ago, a friend's wife was having severe abdominal pain with lots of vaginal bleeding. I prayed and all of the pain left in moments. However, it came back the next day!

I have learned to persevere and growl back at the situation. I rebuked the pain again and it left. But it came back! That happened about five times. She would be better for a while, but it would return.

I was getting discouraged. Someone asked me to pray for her again, but I knew it wouldn't be any good with the current state of my heart on the issue. I could speak the same words but it would be empty this time, with no connection between my heart and my mouth.

I prayed, "God, I know it's your will to heal her, but right now I need you to strengthen my heart. I feel discouraged."

Just a little while after that, a lady told me the testimony of her elderly mother. Her 92-year-old mother had been in the hospital after a stroke, paralyzed on one side of her body and not expected to survive. On the same night we had prayed for the lady with female problems for the first time, we had prayed for the old lady who was in the hospital.

Only now did I learn that soon after we prayed for the old lady, she came home from the hospital with no paralysis, as if she had never had a stroke! That testimony so strengthened my heart and overwhelmed me with God's goodness that I went and prayed for our friend again. This time the pain left completely and never came back. A few weeks later, we were in the pool with our friends. She told us, "This is the first time I've been able to go to the pool for over a year! I couldn't go swimming because I was bleeding so much."

I've had similar experiences many times. It would have been easy to get discouraged, but I kept going and praying for the person again. Sometimes they were healed the fifth time. The natural wisdom that is foolishness to God will twist up your mind and discourage you. It asks numerous questions such as, "If God wanted to heal this person, why didn't he do it last time?" However, when you are strengthened in your inner being by the Holy Spirit and have your mind set on heavenly things, you don't even consider the questions that the earthly-minded, natural man asks.

## *Communion with God*

The word "communion" contains the word "common" within it. You can only have communion with God to the degree you have something in common with him.

The basis for our communion with God is that he is light and now we are light in him. That's what we have in common. Since we are light, scripture exhorts us to walk in the light,[384] put off the deeds of darkness,[385] and have no communion with darkness.[386]

People get demonized and have all kinds of problems by entering into communion with an evil spirit. Teenagers listen to music with suicidal lyrics and become suicidal. Some watch horror movies, develop problems, and need deliverance. Others enter into communion with an antichrist spirit through pornography, and it destroys their families.

## 6. The Heart

People open themselves up to evil spirits in many ways. Then, those spirits manifest in their lives. Spirits are invisible, but they manifest themselves through people who enter into communion with them. God didn't give dominion over the world to angels or spirits; he gave dominion to mankind.[387]

For God's Spirit to manifest through you, break all communion with evil by refusing to rejoice in or entertain anything that the Holy Spirit doesn't rejoice in. Approach God's throne of grace with boldness and confidence,[388] because Jesus has paid the price to make you righteous. Walk in communion with God by rejoicing in what God rejoices in.

We can only understand the things of God by the Spirit of God,[389] and we can have communion with Jesus and the Father because the Holy Spirit dwells in us. When we read a scripture and understand it by the Holy Spirit, our hearts burn with a holy fervor; that's communion with God. When we see someone being healed and we weep with compassion, that's communion with God. When we fill our thoughts with the things of God, our hearts are moved in communion with God.

As we walk in communion with God, we think about what God is thinking about. We care about what Jesus cares about. We laugh with him and weep with him. Do you ever cry because of God's love for people? That is communion with God. Sometimes I pray, "Jesus, here I am. You can weep through me if you want to."

Communion with God is like resonance.[390] Resonance describes the phenomenon in which a tuning fork that is struck will cause another tuning fork of the same pitch to also vibrate. When we immerse ourselves in scripture, testimonies, and heavenly things, we feel the Holy Spirit within us, united with our spirits,[391] resonating in response. It's like something deep within our bellies moving and turning. It may bring tears or laughter. I think of this when I read in scripture, "Deep calls to deep."[392] This resonance with God's Spirit strengthens us and charges us with God's glory.

I watch very little TV and almost never watch movies. Most of it is either boring or repulsive to me. However, I spend hours watching all the Jesus Encounter Ministries meetings and other testimony videos on YouTube. Often when I see what God has done, the tears start pouring out like a river with words in a heavenly language. I feel something deep inside me resonate and I'm swept away in God's river.

That's dangerous to the works of darkness, because my heart is suddenly so consumed by the Lord that I don't care about anything but seeing Jesus. I have no inhibitions, fear of people, or concern for what they think about me. I'm carried away and no longer even consider the condition I confront from a natural point of view. I just see Jesus with the eyes of my heart. Though a person may have had years of chronic pain throughout their whole body, I take their hand and cry out, "Jesus! Jesus!" and it all goes.

## *Waiting on the Lord and Fasting*

God told Israel, "In quietness and rest is your strength." But his people preferred to rely on their own strength instead of on God, so they were defeated![393]

God's power flows from a heart that is at rest in the Lord, yet burning and undivided in agreement with his purposes at the same time. Being still before the Lord is a powerful way to cultivate our hearts and experience communion with God. Some call this "soaking." Become a sponge for God's presence!

You can start with singing to the Lord or reading the Bible. Remind yourself of what Jesus has done for you to position your heart. Then spend time in silence and expectation. You can close your eyes or cover your face to reduce distractions.

This does a few different things. Waiting expectantly on God is an expression of faith and trust. It takes faith to do, and it builds faith. It is an expression of worship, because you give the Lord your full attention. God is a rewarder of those who seek him.[394]

Waiting on the Lord in stillness conditions our hearts to be undividedly focused on the Lord. We choose to focus fully on things above, not on earthly things. We choose to focus not on

## 6. The Heart

what we see or feel, but on what is unseen. We consciously reject anxiety, which is a form of unbelief.

Being still before the Lord eliminates distractions to help us recognize what God is saying. God often speaks in a way that's subtle and seems like one's imagination. It's not so much a matter of whether God is speaking or not, as it is of being tuned into his channel! Spiritual power is released when we hear what God is saying and speak or act in agreement with it, so an important aspect of the mechanics of miracles is recognizing what God is saying.

If you are tuned into many other channels, your mind and heart will be distracted and set on earthly things. You won't have the heavenly perspective in agreement with God that comes from being tuned into his channel.

Stillness may be difficult at first. Your mind wants to wander. Sometimes you'll see all kinds of images flashing before your closed eyes, especially if you've been watching TV! Many people receive so much visual input without ever fully processing it, that when they are finally still their minds start going over everything again. All of that visual noise can hinder you from having eyes to see what God is showing you.

Being still before the Lord is how I've often seen physical conditions that would need healing before I went to a place; and I sometimes know a person's physical condition as soon as I see them. I don't have my eyes closed most of the time when I receive those words of knowledge. However, the time in stillness and darkness helped condition my heart to ignore the distractions and look at what God is seeing, even with my eyes open.

I've spent time waiting on the Lord in silence, and also listening to worship music or the Bible. Often, the time soaking and listening to worship music leads to my heart burning, and then I let what is in my heart burst out through my mouth, praying in human languages or in tongues.

I encourage you to do this regularly. Start with 15 minutes or so and increase it to an hour or even much more! Spending just an hour in dark stillness, not looking or listening to anything natural, is quite an experience.

Jesus and the Apostles in the New Testament also fasted at times. Besides the numerous natural health benefits, fasting is a great way of cultivating the garden of your heart. When we do it with a purpose, it intensifies and purifies our focus. Since we feel weak when fasting, we use times of fasting to cultivate reliance on the Lord and on his power.

Walking with the Lord can sometimes be a real emotional rollercoaster. Our feelings go up and down. Fasting can help to regulate our emotions and not be controlled by them!

The first few days of a fast are usually the hardest, and then it gets much easier. Most healthy people should be able to fast with no problem, but if you are unsure about anything, ask your doctor. I won't say much more about stillness or fasting here because you can find much more extensive information elsewhere.

As a teenager, I used to think of fasting and spending time with God as making a bargain to get more from him! That attitude is harmful because a person who is thinking like that doubts what God has already given us in Christ. A person can easily fast and pray extensively without having a clear revelation of who Jesus is and what Jesus has done for us, and so be powerless. I've seen prayer movements in which most people were relatively powerless for that reason. I also fasted as a teenager but was frustrated because I had never seen God heal people through my hands. I thought the answer was fasting and praying more, but the real problem was that I (and most people around me) had little revelation of Jesus or understanding of the gospel.

When I did start walking in God's power, it was not dependent on fasting. I say that because some people misunderstand and think, "I have to do all of these things in order for God to use me." Then they start trying to measure up in order for God to be able to use them.

That's not how it works! None of us are sufficient in ourselves, but God has qualified us as ministers of the New Covenant![395] In fact, the people who understand the message and see Jesus do miracles through them right away are often

## 6. The Heart

brand-new believers. It's all about Jesus' sufficiency and God freely giving us all things in Jesus. If you think that your discipline or works are what qualify you, that will hinder you from receiving freely what God has for you!

Fasting, waiting on the Lord, and other disciplines don't qualify us, but they are all about cultivating a heart that is undivided, in communion with God, strong in the Lord, and attentive to him. These practices form something inside of us. They do help us to persevere, deal with unbelief and distractions that are limiting us, and grow in the knowledge of Jesus.

I have friends who are a lot more disciplined about their lives than I am, fast a lot more than I do, and spend much more time waiting on the Lord than I do. Some have been caught up and carried from one place to another, as Elijah and Phillip were in the Bible. It's true that I watch very little TV, but that's because walking in God's power is so thrilling that TV is boring to me, not because I'm as disciplined as I could be about my life.

I have a lot of room to grow in Christ. There is so much more, and I need to walk in more, because people need to meet Jesus!

## *Be Strong in the Lord and in the Strength of his Might*

Ephesians tells us to be strong in the Lord.[396] Many scripture references talk about the Holy Spirit strengthening and edifying us in our innermost beings.[397] The apostle John wrote to young men that they were strong and God's word abided in them.[398]

This is how many mighty works happen: God's invisible Spirit strengthens us and then his power flows out of us. God's word is planted in our hearts and grows in us, making us strong inside and edifying us. When our hearts are strengthened by the Holy Spirit and that power is released, God's invisible Spirit manifests through us.

## The Mechanics of Miracles

I've read a few stories of people who were dedicated to Satan from childhood. Those who did so abused them and tore them down, putting them through traumatic rituals, and doing everything possible to break them so as to create a structure for the demonic. People who practice witchcraft have many rituals that they perform in order to connect with certain spirits and gain more power. They give themselves over to evil. What they give themselves over to destroys them!

Satan breaks people down to create strongholds and a soul structure to house demons. The more broken and in bondage the person is, the greater the demonic manifestation that happens through them.

On the other hand, the Holy Spirit builds us up and creates structures in our souls where his power abides.[399] The more built up and free we are in Christ, the greater the manifestation of heaven that flows through our lives.

I know a pastor who was once a crime lord and did black magic. Without giving all the details, he told us of an elaborate ceremony they would do to curse a person. They had to perform many steps in just the right way with just the right words at just the right times. In most cases, the person's body would be filled with tumors and they would die.

However, sometimes a spell would not "stick" if the person targeted had a more powerful spirit. That was sometimes a person who was possessed by more powerful evil spirits, but it was often a Christian walking in communion with the Holy Spirit.

What happens when a warlock casts a curse to make a person sick? His rituals are all about cultivating the heart in spiritual communion. He forms a strong heart-mouth connection. He cultivates and strengthens undivided agreement in his heart with an evil spirit, and then releases what is in his heart through his mouth. Consequently, the spirit he is in communion with manifests in sickness or destruction.

Yet many Christians only timidly pray for the person who was the target of such a curse and say, "God, we know you can heal." Few Christians know how to let their hearts be swept

# 6. The Heart

away by Jesus and let God's glory burst out through their mouths so that God's Spirit, which they are in communion with, manifests in power to bring life.

Power in God's kingdom does not depend on secret knowledge or elaborate rituals as in the kingdom of darkness. We have fullness in Jesus![400] And the Holy Spirit is infinitely more powerful than any spirit of darkness. Yet Christians are often defeated because of ignorance about spiritual things. Few know how to behold God's glory and be strengthened by looking at God through Jesus, not through life.

When everything natural that Abraham saw seemed contrary to God's promise, he didn't waver in unbelief but was strengthened in his faith as he gave glory to God.[401] Many Christians waver in unbelief or explain away God's promises, nullifying his word by their traditions, assuming that God didn't choose to act, instead of understanding God's ways of strengthening us and releasing his power through us. Don't waver! Be strong in the Lord, look at what is unseen, and having done all, stand firm![402]

Few Christians I've met have a heart in undivided agreement with God. Many aren't even sure what God is like or convinced of what God's will is. Few know how to be strong in the Lord and then express that strength by speaking with power and authority. Many are so naturally-minded that they think they are dealing with natural problems and will not even discern when they are confronting spiritual oppression.

Many who belong to the light are ignorant about spiritual things and do not understand how God's invisible Spirit can manifest tangibly through them. They think healing, prophecy, and other manifestations of God's Spirit are just mysterious "spiritual gifts" rather than understanding how these manifestations happen.

Be persistent and radical about opening every area of your life to the Holy Spirit. Give yourself completely to him. Invite him. "Holy Spirit, I welcome your work in every area of my life. If there's any hard-heartedness, draw me, correct me, and I'll come running after you!" Let God's Word correct you.

Pray, "Holy Spirit, show Jesus to me and manifest his nature through me!"

One of the things that most opened me to the Holy Spirit's work in my soul was reconciling with my dad when I was 15 years old and repenting for the times I'd been dishonoring or rebellious towards him. For weeks on end, I was on the verge of tears and thought, "How is it possible for me to love so much? I even love my enemies!" Reconciliation and repentance in human relationships will open you to the Holy Spirit. Is there someone you need to apologize to? Or someone you need to forgive? It may be hard, but the reward is worth it!

## *Use your Tongue to Direct your Heart*

Your tongue is like a rudder that turns your whole life.[403] Use your tongue to direct your heart into the things of God. Read scripture out loud! Thank and praise the Lord with your voice. Tell your soul to bless the Lord![404] Speak God's promises!

One way to be filled with the Holy Spirit is by singing songs, hymns, and spiritual songs.[405] Develop the discipline of praising and thanking God at all times and in every circumstance. Even in terrible circumstances, thank God for what he is accomplishing in the middle of it.[406]

You worship what you are most impressed with. Idolatry is not only loving something else more than you love God, but it is also fearing something more than you are impressed with the Lord.[407] Praise opens the eyes of your heart[408] until you are so impressed with Jesus that everything else looks pitifully puny in comparison with him.

Did you know that to be more impressed with a cancer or other diagnosis than you are with Jesus is idolatry? Are you impressed with the condition or situation, or are you impressed with Jesus? Which is bigger in the eyes of your heart? Is your heart moved by fear because of the situation, or is your heart swept away by God's goodness because you are beholding Jesus with the eyes of your heart?

6. The Heart

Refuse to be more impressed with anything than you are with Jesus Christ. Complaining exalts a problem above God's ability and grace in your life! Cut it out! Refuse to give anything else the attention and awe that Jesus deserves. Praise and thanksgiving make you strong inside and develop faith in your heart.

If you want radical results, be radical. In my early 20's, I wrote scriptures in colored markers on my arms and my house's walls. I praised and thanked the Lord out loud until heavenly and angelic manifestations started happening around me.

## *Let God's Word Expand your Heart*

Do you remember that one of the ways to increase capacitance is to increase the size of the plates? King David wrote that God had enlarged his heart.[409] Nothing is impossible for God,[410] and Jesus said nothing is impossible for him who believes.[411]

God doesn't have limits, but we are limited by what we believe. The Young's Literal Translation of Psalm 78:41 says the Israelites limited God by their unbelief and complaining.

Your internal reality will manifest externally, so let the reality in your heart be formed from communion with God, praise, and thanksgiving. If you want to experience the new normal that God has for you, your heart reality has to change. God's generosity is not limited. God says that if he gave Jesus for us all, he will with him give us all things.[412] But what we receive is often limited by our unbelief.

I've heard that a baby elephant is trained by chaining it to a stake. At first the baby elephant tries to test the limits. But once the elephant learns to give up, he can be tied with a string. Even though he is now a full-grown elephant and could easily break that string or pull up the stake, he won't even try!

Christians are often like that elephant. Even though Jesus has broken all limits for us and God causes us to grow up[413] and become strong[414] by his Spirit, the beliefs we formed in past experiences limit our hearts.

This is true even of Christians who are already walking in power and seeing miracles. I've heard healing ministers say, "That's a rare kind of miracle," regarding healing of autism or another condition. But they are used to spinal problems and certain other conditions being healed.

We never used to hear of steel rods and plates being removed from people's bodies. Now it's common. We used to never hear of bipolar or autism healed. It's becoming increasingly common. We've entered a new normal. Even so, God has far more for us to enter into. He can do far more than we could ever ask or imagine by his power at work within us.[415] Refuse to stay where you are. Refuse to consider anything as difficult. Challenge your own unbelief. Increase your expectation. Push all limits.

Some people minister healing but don't even think to pray for people with glasses or with the common cold, because they are so common! Or they themselves wear glasses! But healing of nearsightedness and colds can also become your new normal in Christ. Challenge what you see with the invisible reality of God's presence.

Since God can do far more than we can ask or imagine, start asking and start imagining. Jesus said if we asked anything in his name, he would do it.[416] I have often started imagining a certain evangelistic situation and I felt God's power tangibly moving through my body with just the thought.

Ephesians 3:21 says, "to God be glory in the church and in Christ Jesus throughout all generations." God is glorified in the church and in Christ because his invisible Spirit takes on flesh in Christ and in his body, the church. God's invisible nature is manifest in the church and in Christ through incarnation. Don't rob God of the glory due him by your unbelief!

If you have clothed yourself with Christ,[417] the members of your body are the members of Christ.[418] When you stretch out your hand, Jesus does. Where your feet take you, Jesus goes! We go to a house and I tell people, "Jesus Christ has come to your house today!"

# 6. The Heart

## *I'm Gonna Explode*

We come to know God's love that surpasses knowledge, seeing God in Jesus, having communion with him through the gift of righteousness, until we are filled with the fullness of God.[419] Now heaven is in our hearts. What is in us is so much bigger than everything outside.

As your heart expands and you're filled with faith and the Holy Spirit, you may begin to feel like you're going to explode. I've walked down the street feeling like that. The pressure inside is so great that I'm about to burst, and it leaks out in tears. What is inside of us is so much bigger than everything outside. When your heart is full of God's glory, prayer is your heart bursting and heaven pouring out.

Have you ever heard someone explode in anger? It's very much like that, but it's God's power, love, and righteousness pouring out. I pray for people like this: "I bless you in Jesus' name! May every one of God's purposes for your life be fulfilled and nothing stand against them! Thank you, God for your goodness soaking into and completely inundating John right now! Holy Spirit, glorify the name of Jesus by your work in John's life!"

As your heart is expanded, God's word and your experience with the Lord are like treasures filling it. When your heart is full of treasure, you can distribute the riches of heaven. You're spiritually rich. You know it and you act like it.

## *Promises for a Walk of Power*

<u>2 Peter 1:3-4 (RSV)</u> His divine power has granted to us all things that pertain to life and godliness, through the knowledge of him who called us to his own glory and excellence, by which he has granted to us his precious and very great promises, that through these you may escape from the corruption that is in the world because of passion, and become partakers of the divine nature.

## The Mechanics of Miracles

As I've prayed and thought about these promises of scripture, I've often begun to feel God's word physically manifest as power on my face and hands. God's word manifests in power when understood and acted on.

The following is my reality. It's full of statements right out of scripture. I'm not going to quote them, but the references are in the endnotes. These Bible promises, applicable to every believer, provide a basis to believe for every single manifestation of God's grace that is listed in 1st Corinthians 12. As you read about them, consider, which promises apply to healing? Which apply to words of knowledge, words of wisdom, miracles, prophecy, the discernment of spirits, tongues, or interpretation of tongues? Which promises apply in general to all of the "grace-effects" and any situation or need we may face?

*I am spiritually rich.[420] Everything I need for life and godliness is available to me in the knowledge of Jesus.[421] I have an abundance of grace and peace in Christ,[422] more than enough to meet my needs and whatever need is before me. If God didn't withhold his own Son, but gave him up for me, how much more will he not also give me all things?[423] God loves me with the same love he has for Jesus and has given me the same glory that he gave to Jesus,[424] in whom the fullness of God dwells bodily.[425] It's that glory that drives out demons, heals the sick, and manifests heaven's reality on earth. I am complete in Christ, lacking nothing.[426] Nothing will be impossible for me if I believe,[427] and God can do immeasurably more than all I can ask or imagine according to his power at work in me.[428] Since I died with Christ[429] and by his resurrection was seated with him in heavenly places,[430] I am in a position of authority over every power[431]: authority to tread on snakes, scorpions, and all the power of the enemy.[432] I have authority over demons and diseases[433] because I've been raised with Christ. I have full access to the Father's presence.[434] The torn body of Jesus is my open heaven,[435] and I have been given every spiritual blessing in heavenly places.[436] Every so-called "spiritual gift" is a spiritual blessing touching and changing the natural world,*

# 6. The Heart

*and there is no spiritual blessing that I don't have access to in Christ.*

*In Jesus are all the treasures of wisdom and knowledge,[437] and he is my wisdom,[438] so I expect wisdom and knowledge from heaven in abundance as I walk in communion with him. I am his sheep, and I hear his voice![439] The gospel is the power (Greek "dunamis") of God for salvation,[440] and I have the gospel! It is the same dunamis that flowed from Jesus and all who touched him were healed![441] The nature of the God I'm in communion with is to heal,[442] and I'm a member of the body of Christ,[443] so his nature is revealed through me! It doesn't matter if you're a finger, a toe, or an arm, the whole body of Jesus, even his cloak, is loaded with healing virtue! Jesus lives in me,[444] and I am in him![445] If Jesus sends me and I go to a house, Jesus Christ is visiting that house.[446] If they receive me, they receive him![447] When I stretch out my hand in obedience to Christ and touch a sick person, Jesus is touching that person!*

These beliefs based on the promises of scripture produce the manifestation of heaven.

## *Push to the Point of Failure*

One way to increase the capacitance of a capacitor is to increase resistance. Anyone who wants to grow or improve wants a challenge.

Bodybuilders grow muscle by pushing to the point of failure. The muscle tears and grows back stronger. That's how they get big. Rather than backing off or trying to explain away powerlessness, challenge yourself to believe God and keep pushing the limits. Believing God honors him. Honor God, and challenge your own unbelief.

This leads us to a place of brokenness. In our weakness God is strong.[448] The brokenness and failure drive us from relying on our strength to relying on the Lord. They lead us to the place of crying out, "Jesus! Help! I can't do this myself!" The apostle Paul said that he was so hard-pressed that it felt like he had received the sentence of death, so that he would not trust in himself but in God who raises the dead.[449]

Brokenness can drive us deep into Jesus to the point where we become dangerous to the works of the enemy, because we immediately give up on our own strength and switch over to letting God manifest his power through us.

Some people see the abundance of miracles in my life and think I'm strong. No. I am weak. I cry out to the Lord and weep! Challenging the limits and failing many times has produced a brokenness, trust, and dependence on God in my heart. I often weep when watching the Jesus Encounter Ministries meetings! Something has been formed in me so that I know I just can't do without a greater manifestation of God's glory.

If you aren't failing, you aren't growing very fast. Be encouraged when you fail, rather than getting discouraged and quitting. I've seen wonderful miracles of tumors and cancer destroyed by God's power. But I've also prayed for people who died, and it hurt! Rather than giving up, I decided to continue honoring God by believing him. I now often just take a person's hand and cry out, "Jesus!" And that is enough. That cry was formed in me through failure.

If God's strength is going to work through you, you need to let go of your mere human ability. Let failure drive you deeper into Jesus Christ. Let it drive your soul into a deep reliance and dependence on the Lord. Your trust gets deeper! The river gets deeper! There are deeper waters! Understand that, instead of trying to explain away failures.

If everyone who touched Jesus was healed,[450] nobody touched him and wasn't healed because they had more issues to work through. Jesus was weak in every way as we are, yet all were healed.[451] There is a point where obstacles just melt before the Lord. Even the rocks and mountains melt.[452] They were hindrances but are no longer.

Even if you have been ministering healing and deliverance for a long time, if your expectation is set at what you've seen before, you are drawing back from walking in faith. Faith sees

## 6. The Heart

the invisible.[453] It is always pushing beyond what you have seen so far. Are you happy with where you are? Or are you still failing and growing?

"I believed, but it didn't work," and Jesus' words, "If you believe, nothing will be impossible for you,"[454] are mutually exclusive statements. Stop thinking of believing as if it were just mental assent.

I received a prophetic word when I was a teenager that I would be like a bodybuilder, becoming strong and lifting heavy weights off people. Those weights include sickness, demonic oppression, broken relationships, broken-heartedness, and more. We want to see heaven's order and deliverance in every area of people's lives.

Is there an area that you haven't seen change? Press in to that area and if you still don't see change, let it produce a cry in your heart to the Lord. Minister to people as often as you can in those situations. Don't accept any affliction as normal.

Did you pray for someone with bipolar disorder and see no change? Look for opportunities to pray for other people with mental health issues. Don't accept mental illness as normal. When your heart is strengthened, minister to that first person again. Press into that area until seeing change in it becomes your new normal.

Be persistent. Persistence is faith, because persistence sees the invisible.

## *A New Normal is a New Heart Reality*

Every experience with God becomes a treasure in our hearts. Our experience with the Lord grows. When our hearts have been in a certain place many times, it is easy to go back there. When we remember what God did before, we feel the same thing we did then, and what was past is now present again in our hearts.

When we've had an experience with the Lord repeatedly, so that our hearts easily revisit the place of prophesying with power, seeing angels, or watching Jesus heal people, we take possession of that territory in the Lord, even as the Israelites took possession of the Promised Land. We lay hold of the riches that are available in Christ.

All of the varied manifestations of God's grace are like this. They are not mysterious superpowers that some people get and some people don't. They are experiences that we grow in. The more we press in and exercise God's grace, the more we grow in it.

Most people who start ministering healing do so after being around someone else who was ministering healing. Many people who exercise discernment of spirits, signs and wonders, prophecy, and other manifestations of God's Spirit began by seeing God's grace work through another person in that area.

Why? Being there when God's grace was manifested through another person gave them a heart experience which they are now able to revisit. That is what we call impartation.

Get around other people who are ministering in God's grace. Rejoice in what God is doing through them, and let your experience with God grow through it. As your experience with God grows, you will often begin to see the same manifestations of the Holy Spirit through your life.

Find people who challenge you! Read the stories and learn from the lives of other people who Jesus has manifested himself through. Let your heart be moved by the testimonies and the desire to see God do such wonders through your life! Follow friends on Facebook who share testimonies on their profiles.

I suggest writing down the testimonies of what God has done in your life and regularly reviewing them. Fill your heart with the wonderful works of Jesus.

I remember a time I wasn't doing well and had trouble forgiving someone. However, when some people invited me to visit a family of unbelievers and pray, all of the sudden my heart was swept away with God's love and it didn't matter what anybody had done to me. Everyone I prayed for received healing.

## 6. The Heart

What happened? Just being in that house and seeing the people triggered me and brought my heart back to many previous experiences. By now, I've had so many experiences with the Lord that this happens quickly. I just hold the hand of someone who is in pain and instantly my heart is burning with God's love but at rest at the same time.

I often say almost nothing, just, "Thank you Jesus." And what I experienced before happens again.

# 7. The Mouth

## *Add your "Amen" to God's "Yes"*

2 Corinthians 1:20 (NIV) For no matter how many promises God has made, they are "Yes" in Christ. And so through him the "Amen" is spoken by us to the glory of God.

God accomplishes his will by speaking his word. All that is visible was created by his word.[455] God made mankind in his image[456] and gave man authority on the earth.[457] He's chosen to accomplish his will on earth through people walking in communion with him and exercising dominion in life.[458] He has given us authority and sent us as ambassadors to speak his word.[459]

All of God's promises are "yes and amen" in Jesus because the invisible God, and mankind with dominion over this earth, are united in Jesus. In Jesus, God's "yes" is joined to the "amen" of a human so that we see the tangible manifestation of the invisible God.

Jesus is the Word of God made flesh.[460] When you understand God's word, believe it in your heart, and speak it with your mouth,[461] the invisible nature of God is also made manifest in your flesh. We are the body of Christ. The Word made flesh is heaven manifest on earth.

Psalm 119:89 says that God has established his word in heaven forever. Psalm 115:16 says the heavens are the Lord's but the earth he has given to the sons of men. God has established his word in heaven and he sends us[462] to establish it on earth. Jesus said nothing would be impossible for us if we believe.[463] Paul said the spirit of faith we have received is, "I believed, and so I spoke."[464] We exercise faith when our heart belief comes out of our mouth.

Just as Jesus exercised dominion in life, scripture says those who receive the abundance of grace and the free gift of righteousness will exercise dominion in life through Jesus.[465] It's simple. Add your "Amen" to God's "Yes."

People doing witchcraft fellowship with an evil spirit, and then agree with that spirit by speaking. Since authority on earth has been given to mankind, and not to angels or spirits, evil spirits look for the agreement of people to be able to do their work. On the other hand, we enter fellowship with God through Jesus and he invites us to join our words with his will so that his Spirit is manifest on earth.

Spiritual fellowship happens in the heart. The spirit a person is in fellowship with manifests when what is in the heart comes out of the mouth. Life and death are in the power of the tongue.[466]

## *The Heart and Mouth Connection*

Out of the abundance of the heart, the mouth speaks.[467] If you confess with your mouth that Jesus is Lord and believe in your heart that God raised him from the dead, you will be saved.[468] Heavenly manifestation works through a heart-mouth connection. You believe, so you speak.[469] God's glory in your heart flows through your mouth.

Scripture says of the prophet Samuel that none of his words fell to the ground.[470] Psalms tells of someone who speaks with a double heart.[471] James said he who is double-minded should not expect to receive anything from the Lord.[472] Many scriptures refer to vain speech.[473] Titus 1:10 refers to "empty talkers." Job 15:3 speaks of "useless talk." The people marveled at Jesus because he spoke as one having authority, not as the pharisees did.[474]

We can speak with power and authority, or our words can fall to the ground. When we have a divided heart or we speak foolishly, our words may fall to the ground. For us to speak

# 7. The Mouth

with Christ's power and authority, our words must flow from a heart that's in undivided agreement with Christ.

Jesus cast out the spirits with a word.[475] In Greek this doesn't mean literally one word, but it means by what he said. Words from heaven flowed through the mouth of the heavenly man,[476] Jesus. Scripture says that God sent out his word and healed them.[477] To see the tangible manifestation, receive that word in your heart, let it resonate with the Holy Spirit within you, and let it burst out of your mouth. Add your "Amen" to God's "Yes."

God's presence manifests through his word. In the Old Testament as they sang, "The Lord is good and his love endures forever," God's presence manifested tangibly so that the priests could no longer stand to minister.[478] When we praise God from the heart, God's invisible nature that we are singing or boasting about manifests tangibly. God is enthroned on the praises of his people.[479] Heaven's dominion on earth comes through praise.

In the Old Testament, God fought for the Israelites and gave them victory over a million-man army as they thanked and praised him.[480] In the New Testament, the chains fell from Paul and Silas, and they were released from prison as they praised and thanked the Lord.[481] We are filled with the Holy Spirit as we sing psalms, hymns, and spiritual songs, giving thanks in our hearts to the Lord.[482]

Since God gave authority on the earth to mankind, not to angels, many angels are eager to minister but they are waiting for a person who will partner with God's purposes on earth by adding their "Amen" to God's "Yes." Angels act in response to God's word.[483]

When you share a testimony, angels take that as God's word and as your agreement with God. As we boast in the Lord, going on and on talking about Jesus and what he has done, angelic activity becomes apparent. People get healed without anyone even praying for them. They sometimes feel a wind blow over them or a hand touching them. Signs and wonders follow.

Psalms 86 speaks of having an undivided heart that fears God's name, so as to praise God with a whole heart.[484] Several other psalms refer to praising God with a whole heart.[485] Psalm 103 says, "Bless the Lord oh my soul, and all that is within me, bless his holy name."[486] That is the heart-mouth connection in praise.

What moves your heart? I have triggers. Some worship songs move me. Often, I'm all tears and God's love sweeps my heart away when I get to certain lyrics. They might be, "All for love the Savior died," or, "Jesus, I give you everything." My own memories and other people's stories of what God has done also trigger that place of undivided fervency in my heart.

Read books about historical revivals. Listen to accounts of revival on YouTube. Create a playlist of your favorite worship songs. Immerse yourself in the things of God, and you will find triggers that bring your heart to a place of undivided fervency before the Lord.

When you find a trigger that moves your heart, stay in that place as long as you can. If you broke down in tears listening to a worship song, keep playing that song again! If it was a scripture, write that scripture down and keep going back and thinking about it. If it was a testimony, keep telling that testimony to more people. If it was a story about revival, listen to it again. Then let what is in your heart burst out of your mouth in praise and thanksgiving to God.

## *Say What you Mean and Mean What you Say*

Through many experiences of praying for people, my ability to sense that heart-mouth connection has increased. I often know the person is healed before I even ask them because I feel the connection between my heart and my mouth. There have been other times when I know I'm struggling. I'm saying words, but they feel empty.

I often feel power flowing from my heart through my mouth even when there is no physically tangible manifestation.

# 7. The Mouth

I also feel when there's a disconnect between my heart and my words.

Several things can break or weaken that heart-mouth connection. It's important to keep your words coming from your heart. People who flatter others or lie create a heart-mouth disconnect. They are saying something that they know in their heart isn't true.

Walk in integrity, and speak the truth. Never joke foolishly with hurtful or impure words and then say, "I didn't mean it," or, "it was just a joke." If you want your words to have spiritual power and not fall to the ground, then take seriously what you say. Your mouth is a powerful weapon, so use it for life and not for death.

Don't make commitments lightly. Rarely make promises. If you do, be careful to follow through. Only say you are going to do something if you know you will. If you don't take your own word seriously, how do you expect it to be taken seriously in the spiritual world? Many people say they will donate to a ministry or do something for someone and they never follow through. It's better to just not promise anything, and then when you are ready to do what was in your heart, do it.

I saw a situation in which a person was upset because she prayed for someone with cancer and the cancer wasn't healed. However, she lived in anger, complaining, negativity, and depression. I heard her getting furious with someone and say, "I'll kill you!" I heard her saying, "He can go to hell." She also made many negative comments about herself. It's a mercy that some Christians' words are not fulfilled! It's a mercy that they don't walk in spiritual authority! They would do much more harm than good by what they say!

## *Exercising Authority*

Jesus' death broke Satan's power and Jesus' resurrection raised us up to a place of authority. There is only one level of authority in Christ, and it is "seated with Christ in heavenly places, far above all power and authority."[487]

# The Mechanics of Miracles

We exercise that power and authority to the extent that we walk in identification with Jesus' death and resurrection. This means really believing we have died and risen with Christ, and acting accordingly! I call this being in a gospel position.

Let's give some examples. The first is a person who is addicted to pornography and needs deliverance from a spirit of lust. Is your conscience clean in that area? If it isn't, shame is affecting you. You won't be able to speak out of an undivided heart because you have an area of agreement with the spirit you are rebuking. You can rebuke the spirit, but you're lacking the heart-mouth connection. Your heart isn't fully in agreement with what is coming out of your mouth, so your words fall to the ground. To walk in authority, you must bring that area of darkness into Christ's light and let Jesus' blood cleanse your conscience so that you have no agreement with darkness.

Identifying with Jesus' death and resurrection involves believing that you have died to sexual immorality and been raised with Christ in newness of life.[488] The power comes from identifying with Jesus' death, and the authority comes from identifying with Jesus' resurrection.

Another situation is that of someone with cancer. What is filling your heart and motivating your prayer? Are you praying because you're afraid they might die, or because Jesus' glory overwhelms you and you want to express it?

Jesus broke the power of the devil by his death,[489] so if you are in identification with Jesus' death and your heart is in a gospel position, you will fear no evil.[490] But if you fear cancer, cancer moves your heart and you no longer are speaking out of an undivided heart when you rebuke cancer. You don't have the full heart-mouth connection.

It is a form of idolatry to fear or be impressed with anything more than we are impressed with our God and his goodness.[491] The cure for idolatry is true worship. The cure for fear is worship. To fear the Lord and be totally impressed with him destroys other fears. His perfect love casts out fear.[492]

Another example is that of ministering to a person who worships demons. Do you remember the story of how I prayed

## 7. The Mouth

and released God's goodness on a man who worshipped spirits, not even knowing what he was involved in, and those spirits crawled to the closet on their hands and knees and surrendered, throwing their witchcraft articles on the floor?

That religion and similar ones involve many sacrifices and offerings. People live in fear of spirits, and sacrifice to those spirits to gain their blessing or escape their curse. That is of the antichrist spirit, which puts something else in the place of Jesus Christ and the redemptive work of his death and resurrection.

How are you going to confront the antichrist spirit of false religion if you live your Christianity in the same way? If your motivation for putting money in the offering is to somehow gain more of God's blessing than you have in Christ (implying we have not really been given every blessing in heavenly places by Jesus' resurrection), or to escape a curse (implying Jesus' blood wasn't sufficient to break every curse), you're thinking in the same way as that person in false religion is!

If you are in agreement with an evil spirit, how will you exercise authority over it? Any area of agreement in your heart with an evil spirit can break the heart-mouth connection necessary to exercise authority over it. You can rebuke it, but your words feel empty and fall to the ground.

When you don't have the heart-mouth connection, it comes back to tending the garden of your heart, fellowship with the Lord, and rooting up the weeds. Repent! Apply the gospel! Change the way you think! Fully agree with God!

## *Immunity to Witchcraft*

I've sometimes helped people who were being attacked by witchcraft. Because what I share with them goes back to the basics of the gospel, I've thought of doing an evangelistic seminar called "How to be immune to witchcraft." It's essentially, "Here's the gospel. Believe it, enter into communion with Jesus, and break communion with Satan."

Jesus told his disciples that they would trample on snakes, scorpions, and over all Satan's power, and nothing would harm them.[493] That's not to say Christians can't be attacked by witchcraft. The protection isn't automatic, coming only by having raised your hand once to accept Jesus. We walk in that protection by living in communion with God's Spirit and by our present faith in Jesus' victory.

Evil spirits try to get the Christian to agree with them in some way in order to attack them. That could be simply by getting you to fear so that you give them the attention only Jesus deserves. Witchcraft often finds a vulnerability when the person who is cursed reacts in the same spirit as the one doing witchcraft against them.

For example, someone had a cruel and angry boss who we believed was involved in witchcraft. The employee came home with a sharp pain in the kidneys and believed she had kidney stones. But I prayed and rebuked it and a spirit came out with loud belches. After several loud belches, the pain was gone.

The boss had screamed at her that day. When she reacted in anger, her kidneys started to hurt. She became vulnerable to spiritual attack when she reacted in the same spirit that her boss was walking in. Like Dan Mohler says, "Don't let sin against you produce sin in you!" By reacting hatefully to her boss, she had ventured into the dominion of darkness that Jesus redeemed us from![494]

Everything was fine for several months after casting out the spirit. Then one day, she returned from work with terrible kidney pain again and was complaining that she had to go to the doctor. Again, her boss had screamed at her and her heart reaction was hatred.

I thought, "Don't you realize that this is a spiritual attack, not a physical issue? It left as a spirit the first time, and now the same thing happened that let that spirit in the first time, and you have pain again!"

She kept complaining about the pain and I suddenly spun around and said, "You spirit attacking her kidneys, get out right now in Jesus' name!" Deep, loud belches came out for a minute and all the pain was gone.

# 7. The Mouth

I said, "You need to protect yourself spiritually. Guard your heart so that you don't get pulled into the darkness that your boss is living in. If you come into agreement with a dark spirit, you become vulnerable to it attacking you."

Loving people so much that you no longer fear them makes you immune to witchcraft attacks. The Holy Spirit who is in us is greater than everything else.[495] Walking in victory is a matter of communing with God and letting him manifest himself through us.

Jesus' teachings to love our enemies, bless those who curse us, and do good to those who hate us,[496] are keys to being immune to witchcraft. When people who are in darkness manifest whatever spirit they have connected to, refuse to react in the same spirit. Instead, let the Holy Spirit manifest through you.

It's sad that so many Christians are afraid of witchcraft. Knowing how to respond to it is fundamental. It's extremely common in Brazil. Many Christians are not getting the most basic teaching that they need to deal with what they confront.

A leader from one of the local churches took me to pray for a lady with cancer. She was telling me that the atmosphere was so demonic the previous time that she got sick. I went, didn't even notice any dark atmosphere, and later we heard the lady was cancer-free. Then, we went to her daughter's hair salon, and Jesus healed the customers. The daughter had previously been healed of a tumor causing intense pain in her head.

The lady who took me to pray felt that it was so dark because, even though she was a Christian, she still thought in some ways like a person who does witchcraft. She was impressed with the devil, not with Jesus' victory, so the spirit there affected her, and she felt sick. Worship Jesus until he's so big in the eyes of your heart that everything else looks puny. Then, your heart reality will determine the atmosphere around you.

## *Fervency and Rest*

Anxiety in your heart will also break the heart-mouth connection. Hebrews exhorts us to strive to enter God's rest, for whoever does so rests from his own work.[497]

James says that the fervent prayer of a righteous person is powerful.[498] Righteousness has to do with a heart in communion with God, and fervency means "burning." The heart-mouth connection is there when you have a heart that is burning with God's presence and you are at rest in the Lord at the same time. God's power flows when you speak out of a heart in that position.

People who've been in church for a long time often try too hard when they pray for healing. They are worried about saying all the right words and praying long enough to be "spiritual." They take more time than necessary and feel pressure to perform. This hinders the heart-mouth connection. But I often grab brand-new believers, tell them what to do, and God's power flows through them tremendously! Why? Like babies, they don't have any expectations to live up to! They are at rest, not striving.

I often see God's power flow through me easily when I'm hanging out with people and having a good time. I'm relaxed, and I start praying for everyone. I'm so bold that some people think I'm crazy, but I don't care what they think, so I'm not under pressure. I grab other people and get them to pray. That's fun for me!

Another situation in which I see a tremendous flow of God's power is when I preach and have everyone minister to each other. My heart gets swept away as I'm sharing God's word, and tears flow as I share the testimonies. Often, people are healed before we even pray.

Then, I do everything I can to get the people to pray for each other even if they feel inadequate. I tell them to keep it simple, to add their "Amen" to God's "Yes," and to pray with authority and thanksgiving. I only pray for a few people myself. Everyone tests the condition and we evaluate what

## 7. The Mouth

happened. Then everyone prays again for any who need more prayer. After that, if anyone is left with a pain or symptom, I pray for them and invite everyone else to pray with me.

More happens in that way than would happen if I prayed for everyone myself, and it's so much easier. It takes the pressure off of me. I'm not trying to perform. I'm just letting the Holy Spirit work through God's word. God does the work and God gets the glory! I just jump in the river and let it carry me.

In both of these situations, I've sometimes seen 100% of the people healed before leaving, and often nearly 100%. (To the best of our ability to evaluate.)

However, I think about how often I was stressed and felt a disconnect between my heart and mouth while praying for people on the phone. I have experienced tremendous miracles by praying for people through social media or over the phone. However, I sometimes still struggle when praying on the phone. I feel stressed. I've been asking the Lord to help me, because when I feel that disconnect, the results are not the same.

Then I realized that I feel people's expectation when I pray on the phone because in most cases, they contacted me because they read testimonies. I feel pressure to live up to their expectations and so I feel stressed. If that happens, it breaks the heart-mouth connection in which the words flow directly from what's filling my heart. Instead of a single heart burning with God's presence, anxiety gets mixed in. It doesn't feel the same as praying for some person on the street who thinks I'm crazy anyways and I might never see again.

I already threw away my reputation in order to have the courage to pray so boldly for the non-religious person on the street! Become of no reputation, let Jesus do the work, and let Jesus get the glory!

Another trigger of fervency in my heart is holding the hand of the person I'm praying for. I've prayed for so many people that way and come back in tears over what I saw Jesus do. The moment I hold the person's hand and stand back, it feels like I'm reliving those previous experiences. Sometimes, I'm praying for someone on the phone and I feel like, "I wish I could just hold their hand."

God isn't limited by distance, but sometimes our own hearts are limited. We need the Lord to help us expand our hearts[499] and break every limitation in our belief and expectation. I have friends who've experienced a lot more miracles over the phone than I have!

Mark Hemans often tells a person receiving prayer, "Close your eyes. I can't help you." He is taking the expectation and pressure off himself and letting the Lord do it. His part is just agreeing with God and trusting him.

Sending WhatsApp messages and Facebook messages more often when praying for people, rather than calling them, has helped me. God has no limitations, but it is sometimes easier for me to relax and let the fervency in my heart flow out through my mouth when I send a voice message, instead of being worried about the result so as to feel an expectation on myself that I can never meet.

We rely fully on the Lord and can do nothing in ourselves! His grace is abundant! We have to rest from our own works to let his grace flow.

A friend who ministers powerfully on the street and in daily life shared about her first time ministering as a guest speaker at a church. Almost nothing was happening at first! For her, that was the situation in which she felt stressed; like she had to live up to some kind of expectation for guest speakers. It broke the heart-mouth connection! She had to relax for God's power to flow. God's power flows through a heart positioned in humility that isn't trying to prove anything.

This sometimes comes into play when ministering to family members. Many people feel the heart-mouth connection broken when ministering to close friends and family members because they are stressed about the situation. So, I'm explaining the spiritual dynamics of what is happening in such situations in order to help you cultivate your heart and enter a new normal in Christ.

## 7. The Mouth

On several occasions, I've prayed for myself for healing and didn't notice any change, but when I was relaxing, having a good time, and praying for other people, God's power came on me and healed me. I needed to relax! How could I have prayed for some people five different times on different days and the fifth time they were healed? In some cases, it was because the fifth time I was relaxed and having a good time! Stop trying so hard and let God's river flow!

Similarly, someone may flow tremendously in prophecy to a stranger on the street...but then, in another situation, they feel the pressure of expectation on them and they lose the heart-mouth connection! As you grow in experience with feeling God's power flow through you, you can also sense when something is interfering with that connection between your mouth and your heart.

Some ministers, including John Mellor and Roger Sapp, might tell a joke when ministering healing. It breaks the tension. People who've been in church for a long time often try way too hard! They pray much more than they need to! It's often easier for teenagers or brand-new Christians to minister healing with power than it is for people with a long religious history.

## *Your Actions Must Accompany your Words*

A big problem for many religious people is that they get used to repeating creeds but acting as if they weren't true. They say, "Jesus heals," but they don't lay hands on the sick. They won't even pray for a backache or headache, because they have no expectation.

Remember my story of being on the prayer mountain and everyone was prophesying that a woman would be healed, but nobody asked her to test her body after? Their prophecies were empty words. It was obvious they had no expectation, which is why they said, "You will be healed" (at some undefined future time) rather than, "Thank you, Jesus, for healing her now!"

Remember the preacher prophesying, "People will get out of wheelchairs in this church," but I didn't see anybody laying hands on the guy in a wheelchair? If you say something, but act as if it's not true, you don't have the heart-mouth connection, so your words are empty. Mental assent to doctrine divorced from action is not faith.

I've heard a lot of preachers screaming and "prophesying" but there's no power. It's just empty words. Unfortunately, a lot of Christians confuse that with the anointing in the culture that I'm in!

Real fervency can be expressed quietly or loudly. Sometimes I yell, rebuking that which is hurting a person, blessing them intensely, agreeing with what God wants for their life. Sometimes I take their hand and whisper, "Jesus! Jesus! Jesus!" Whether loud or quiet, what matters is a heart on fire and fully in agreement with the Lord's purposes.

## *Don't Just Minister out of Routine*

In São Paulo, I was having a tremendous time praying for people from morning until late at night. I preached at a church in which I couldn't find a single person who still hadn't received the healing they needed. Then, they asked me to pray for impartation.

I hadn't been emphasizing impartation so much but I probably needed to emphasize it more. I prayed for everyone again at their request. Some people started sobbing with compassion as God's glory came on them. Several people fell. A few collapsed as if they were struck by lightning as I stretched my hand out from a distance. I knew it was the Lord. Although it's precious to me when God touches people in that way, I previously had not often seen people fall when I prayed.

Someone gave me a ride to the hotel room. I shut the door, and I started weeping, raising my hands, and thanking God for what he did. Thanksgiving and praise poured out like a river! I was so humbled, overwhelmed, and grateful to God for the

## 7. The Mouth

undeserved riches he gave me in Christ and his wonderful work in my life.

I was tired and going to take a nap and go swimming before ministering at the next church a few hours later. However, about twenty minutes later, the guy who'd given me a ride to the hotel returned and asked if I'd be willing to pray for some people at his pharmacy.

I said, "Sure!" He took me to the pharmacy and God healed his employees. One started sobbing. I saw into her body by the Holy Spirit and told her God was healing a blood condition that she hadn't even mentioned. It was glorious!

I was back at the hotel for about 40 minutes and took a nap before it was time to go to the next church. I'd been going non-stop, and all that was happening was so overwhelming that when they lined up people to receive prayer after the message, I wasn't feeling the heart-mouth connection anymore.

I went down the line praying for every person. Yet it felt like my words were empty, rather than feeling power flowing up from my heart through my mouth. I was just saying the same words again. I'd been going for so long, I was emotionally exhausted, and it felt like rote! I was struggling and not much was happening.

I said, "Jesus, help me!" At about the middle of the line, my heart began to be moved with love for the people. The connection was back! They had lined up to receive prayer for impartation, not specifically for healing. But I stopped at one guy and said, "You need healing, don't you?" He replied, "Yes." I tapped his stomach and said, "Right here, isn't it?" The pastor said, "Wow!" The man had a chronic stomach problem and nobody had told me about it.

On the last day of the trip, something similar happened. A Christian brother had one leg shorter than the other. We prayed for him for a while, but then I interrupted and ran across the street to pray for the guy with a crutch whose story we already shared. He left swinging his crutch an hour later.

We returned to praying for the first man, who had felt some improvement before but still had some pain and a shorter leg. I wasn't feeling the heart-mouth connection. I was doing my best to pray but my words felt empty, like I was just repeating the same things I'd been saying all weekend. So, I asked the pastor to pray! The pastor prayed with authority and the man was healed. I knew it was no good for me to keep praying for him until my heart was ready.

In both cases, I was so elated by what God previously did that I was coming off an emotional high that exhausted me, and I fell into routine. Your emotions may go wild when walking with the Lord, up and down, and you need his help to stay stable and steadfast regardless of your emotions!

It will help you to be aware of the state of your heart and to learn to prepare your heart to minister to people. Get your heart burning! I prepare my heart by speaking in tongues and thinking about the Lord, his Word, and his mighty works before I go out. I've also heard Mark Hemans mention preparing his heart to minister, and I'm sure other ministers relate.

## *The Heart-Mouth Cycle*

Your mouth is like a rudder directing your heart,[500] and what is in your heart comes out of your mouth.[501] What you speak in power manifests around you in life or death[502] and affects your experience.

Many people live in a vicious heart-mouth cycle. Doubt flows from the mouth of a person with a heart of unbelief. This may manifest as complaining or as human doctrines of unbelief invented to explain their experience. People caught in that cycle live a life of spiritual poverty and barrenness. They think as if God were stingy. They use their experience that is the result of their unbelief to confirm their unbelief. Even when God clearly intervenes in a situation, they are blind to see it because they are not thankful,[503] so they soon forget what God has done.

Bitterness and curses come from a heart of anger and unforgiveness, and this produces more strife and problems.

## 7. The Mouth

The person caught in this cycle then becomes more bitter because of what their words have produced.

You can repent, let Jesus set you free from the vicious cycle, and instead enter a virtuous heart-mouth cycle. This starts with praise and thanksgiving in all circumstances[504] and with studying the works of the Lord.[505] Fill your heart with testimonies and with God's promises from scripture.[506] Praise and thanksgiving are the eyes with which you see Jesus. A person who refuses to be thankful is spiritually blind.

This life of praise and thanksgiving, especially when combined with actions of faith, produces miracles. When you see what God does, it deepens the gratitude and awe that pours out of your mouth in more praise, thanksgiving, and worship. This stirs up angelic activity around you. Angels are ministering spirits sent by God,[507] but they are waiting for people to add their "Amen" to God's "Yes."[508]

This virtuous cycle of praise, thanksgiving, and miracles is a new normal that goes beyond what many people could even imagine. It's a life of faith in every circumstance. It's a life in which you experience the riches of heaven and the generosity of the Father who gave his only Son for us and said that he would also give us all things with Jesus.[509] You experience more than you could have asked or imagined by God's Spirit working in you.[510]

In this cycle of praise, thanksgiving, and miracles, you feel God's love and goodness pursuing you. You live in joyful expectation. You see prayers answered before you even finish praying them.[511] Sometimes you are struck mute in awe of the Lord. All you can do is bow before the Lord, weep, and thank him.

You boast in the Lord[512] all day long, and his praise is continuously in your mouth.[513] It becomes your experience that "If I were to recount your wonders, Lord, they would be more than can be numbered."[514] Rivers of living water flow from your innermost being.[515] This is normal Christianity. It's the new normal that God is inviting the church to enter.

# 8. God's Grace Manifests through Faith

I've focused mostly on the spiritual dynamics of how God's grace manifests supernaturally through us. That is, seeing the invisible God through Jesus and his redemptive work, cultivating our hearts with the reality of God's presence, and then releasing that heart reality through our mouths so that God's invisible nature is manifest tangibly. There has been a big lack of teaching these simple and fundamental truths.

I've been hearing from some people who've learned the right doctrine about healing and wonder why it doesn't seem to be working for them. They have the doctrine in their minds but they still don't have a single, undivided heart. Increase comes from growing in the experiential knowledge of Jesus, not from doctrine or how-to. For God's power to flow through truth, you have to understand in your heart and disconnect from being moved by what you see naturally.

Some practical advice and tips may help you to step out in faith. They don't do any good without having communion with God through Jesus, but when you are walking in communion with God, they can help you to partner with him.

## *Tongues and Interpretation*

When I was baptized in the Holy Spirit, I expected God to just take control of my mouth. Yet I didn't speak in tongues at that moment, so I thought I hadn't received. Soon after, I started randomly yelling out gibberish. I thought I was just being a crazy teenager, but after a while I started to wonder if I was really speaking in tongues. The youth pastor encouraged me to continue. I walked home speaking in that language the whole way. I felt so much peace that I knew it was God.

Missionary Jackie Pullinger shares that when she first spoke in tongues she was embarrassed and didn't feel anything, so she didn't do it again. Then some Americans told her, "The Bible doesn't say you will feel edified! It says you will be edified." She started speaking in tongues regularly.

Instead of saying, "God, I'm going to talk to that person. Please help me!" she would ask God to lead her to the person whose heart he was preparing. She finally began to see people giving their lives to Jesus!

The drug addicts would give their lives to Jesus, come to live at her mission, and learn to speak in tongues. They spoke in tongues until they fell asleep and had no withdrawal symptoms.[516]

I've talked to people who spoke in tongues once and then never did again. They felt foolish. Some people help others to speak in tongues by saying, "repeat after me" or telling them to praise God until they run out of words and another language comes out. As foolish as these exercises may sound, they have helped some people!

It takes faith to speak in tongues, and it challenges the natural way of living by feelings and trusting only a visible reality. Speaking in tongues builds up and strengthens your heart. If you've spoken in tongues before but stopped, start doing it again! It's not about what you feel. Do it by faith because the Bible says it edifies you.[517]

Once I met a guy whose mentor taught him to speak in tongues for 8 hours a day. He could see a person and if they had 20 physical problems in their body, he would describe in detail what those problems were by revelation from the Holy Spirit. He encouraged me, so I spoke in tongues for the whole 8-hour drive to Toronto where I was going to preach. I started to experience the same.

Since speaking in tongues edifies your heart and strengthens the heart-mouth connection, it is a gateway into

## 8. God's Grace Manifests through Faith

many other manifestations of God's grace. It's great to combine it with reading scripture, praise, and worship. Since it comes from your spirit, not your mind, you can do it at the same time as you read the Bible!

Praying in tongues conditions you to look past the natural situation and go beyond your emotions to see what God is doing and hear what God is saying. Since your tongue is like a rudder and the Holy Spirit speaks through us when we pray in tongues,[518] praying in tongues helps steer us in the direction God has for us.

Interpretation is not translation. It's isn't usually word-for-word, but it's the idea of what's being said. Interpretation of tongues also works by faith. You speak in tongues and your heart gets filled with something to speak in a human language. Interpretations of tongues are often simple and right out of the Bible. They can be specific, but they also often sound like general, sound, scriptural words of encouragement, filled with praise to God. They come with great power. You may feel foolish, your heart pounding as if you're going to jump out of an airplane when you feel that you have a prophecy in tongues or interpretation in tongues. Just do it!

A few months ago, at our men's meeting, I was speaking in tongues and felt something burning in my heart. When there was an opportunity, I spoke up loudly in tongues and then gave an interpretation. It was something like, "God says 'Yield your lives to me and I will make the members of your bodies members of righteousness so that you will go out and the spirit of Jesus will be manifest in this city through you!'"

The message was simple and it took faith to speak up. After I gave it, my body was physically vibrating with God's power in a way that was stronger than I'd felt in over a year, and I got weak and fell backwards into a chair. Great power is released when you hear from God and then say what he is saying.

## Hearing, Feeling, and Seeing in the Spirit

God speaks in many ways. Although God may speak audibly, it's important to understand that sometimes his voice is subtle and may seem like our imagination.

Test what you are sensing, and remember that other people are also supposed to test your revelation.[519] Many prophecies are easy to test with scripture. Spend plenty of time reading the Bible because doing so is communion with the Holy Spirit and helps you to recognize God's voice.

Sometimes, testing prophecies and words of knowledge is a matter of confirming if they are true or not for that situation. For example, I passed a lady on the street and in my mind's eye, I saw myself praying for her kidneys. We already know it's biblical that God wants to heal people. So, to test a word like that, ask about her kidneys.

She had kidney problems, so the word was accurate. Just like speaking in tongues felt foolish, asking a stranger about her kidneys feels foolish. But we act in faith, and our desire to see the mighty works of Jesus is greater than our fear of embarrassment!

Our team was praying for the guys at the recovery house during worship. As I approached a man who had recently arrived, the thought came, "He has a stone in his body." I didn't have any impression of where it might be. Because the music was so loud, I yelled. "You have a stone in your body! Is that right?"

He yelled back, telling me how bad the situation was. The doctors said he could die if it wasn't resolved, and he needed surgery. The stone was in his gallbladder.

I said, "Who told me about the stone? You didn't tell me. I just told you, and you confirmed it." Realizing that I was the one who brought up the stone, he was confused. "I don't know." I continued, "Jesus told me about the stone, because he is removing it right now, and you won't need that surgery." I prayed, he felt heat, the pain left, and he stood up and testified."

## 8. God's Grace Manifests through Faith

I started by getting words of knowledge for healing for somebody nearby. I didn't know who it was specifically. Most of those words came by feeling a vibration, heat, or even wind touch part of my body. It was often a subtle sensation but proved to be accurate. Some people describe receiving words of knowledge by momentarily feeling a pain that is not their own. Ask God to speak to you, pay close attention to what you feel and sense, and have the courage to act on it and not be afraid to fail! Sometimes you'll feel something at the moment you look at or think about a specific person. You'll grow in words of knowledge with practice!

God also speaks in many other ways. I've often had a thought come to me or a vision when I ask God to speak. It's hard to describe but it's like I'm looking through the natural realm and I see something flash before my eyes in an instant. That is how I often know who has a specific condition.

I could describe it as God's love filling my heart and then his love sees into the person and sees what their problem is. At the men's group I saw, in my mind's eye, God's power ripping the desire for pornography out of a young guy's belly and chest. I asked, "Is porn a problem in your life." He said, "Yes." I described what I saw God doing. We prayed and he felt tremendously relieved, as if a weight had been lifted off him.

You may give words of knowledge by praying for a specific situation you had no natural knowledge about. One man at the recovery house asked me to pray for him, but didn't have a specific request. As I prayed, the words flowed, "Thank you God for your power on his teeth! Restore his teeth, Lord, in Jesus' name! Every infection, get out now!"

After prayer, he told me that he had a tooth which was broken and in pain. He couldn't drink anything hot or cold, and he believed he needed a root canal. When I prayed, he felt vibration and numbness in his mouth. The pain left. Two weeks later, he recorded his testimony. He had not had any problem with his tooth since then. Jesus gave him a root canal!

As I was praying for a pre-teen with an autoimmune disease, I saw God's glory touching her eyes. I prayed, "Thank you God, for your glory on her eyes! In Jesus' name, every spirit affecting her vision, get out! In Jesus' name, vision be restored." She was not wearing glasses, and nothing natural indicated a vision problem.

After prayer, I asked what she felt. She'd felt a shiver and the pain had left her body. Then I said, "Maybe you noticed that I prayed for your eyes, because I saw God's glory touching your eyes. Does that make sense to you? Were you having any problems with your vision?"

She started to say, "Yes, it makes sense. I can't see clearly." But as she was finishing the sentence, she looked across the room, went mute, and dropped her face into her hand, sobbing. We asked, "What's happening?" She replied, "I'm seeing clearly."

Walking in communion with God is what's most important, but there are some prophetic "exercises" that may seem foolish, but help us to recognize God's voice. One is to first prepare your heart by thinking of God's love for the person you are praying for. Then ask God to speak to you, and imagine you are putting your hand in a brown paper bag and pulling something out.[520] What did you take out of the bag? Ask God what it symbolizes for the person you are praying for.

You may feel like, "I don't know if I'm just making this up, or if it's really God." Share what you saw, and what you believe it meant. This should be coherent with God's nature and his love for the person. Then ask for their feedback. Was it relevant to them? Did they feel that the Holy Spirit confirmed it?

We make it clear when we do this exercise that we are growing in God's grace, and the words must be tested and confirmed by the Holy Spirit to the person receiving. Don't be afraid of missing it. I don't know anybody who learned to walk or ride a bike without falling.

I have repeatedly seen people who never prophesied before surprised at the accuracy of words they received from the Lord when they did the paper bag exercise. Some words were so accurate and specific that there was no possibility of coincidence. God frequently speaks by giving thoughts and

## 8. God's Grace Manifests through Faith

pictures on the screen of our mind as we commune with him, but people often don't recognize this as God speaking, at first. Those images seem like their imagination.

Some people have difficulty with this exercise. They've been told that Christians should not trust or listen to our hearts, because the Bible says the heart is deceitful and desperately wicked.[521] However, they forget that this scripture describes the unregenerate heart. The Bible says that in the New Covenant God gives us a new heart and a new spirit, removing the heart of stone, giving us a heart of flesh, and putting his Spirit in us![522] The heart is now the dwelling place of the Holy Spirit! Those who are telling Christians, "Don't listen to your heart" are in error.

We still need to guard our hearts and submit them to God's word, but God does speak to our hearts! You should listen to your heart when your heart is in communion with God, filled with his love and his Word! Test what you hear or feel. Abide in God's Word, and let it abide in you.[523]

You will never get to a point where you don't need faith anymore! After so many experiences, I'm still often not sure if I'm hearing God. But acting in faith on a slight impression can bring tremendous results! Last Friday, I was at a pizza place and I saw the left shoulder of the manager highlighted in my mind's eye. I thought, "Am I imagining this?" but I asked and she had shoulder pain, so I said, "Jesus is healing you." I took her hand, said, "Thank you Jesus," asked her to test it, and the pain was gone.

A little while later I went up to her and said, "You know, if other people here need healing too, we can pray for them and Jesus will heal them." She had everyone who worked at the pizza place get prayer. All but two had pain in their bodies, some severe. It was gone instantly when I took their hands, thanked God, and rebuked the pain. Everyone who had glasses could see clearly without glasses after prayer. We prayed, they felt heat and something move in their eyes, and their vision improved. We prayed again a second or third time and let the heat of God's power seep in until they tested their eyesight and said it was 100%.

We were loudly praising and thanking Jesus in the pizza place. None of that would have happened without acting in faith on a slight impression and having a heart prepared with an aggressive attitude of, "I want to see Jesus tonight!"

Often in life, I've acted in self-reliance according to what seemed best to me and it didn't turn out well. So, I'm learning to rely on God and on his voice. Just a whisper can change everything. His power is in his word.[524] If you need wisdom, ask God what to do. Just do what he says.[525] If you put your hope in the Lord and in his voice, you won't be disappointed! Provision is in his voice. Breakthrough is in his voice.

Waiting on the Lord quietly and asking him to speak to you is an expression of trust in him.[526] Stop, let the static die down, and tune in to God. Quiet your heart[527] and trust in him.[528] Pay close attention to what you see, hear, and feel when the noise is gone. God promises to give wisdom to those who ask in faith![529]

Because God frequently speaks symbolically, reading your Bible often helps to understand what a vision means. The Bible uses lots of symbolism. If you don't understand a vision you saw, keep thinking about it and ask God to make the meaning clear to you. The interpretation sometimes comes with time. I wrote a whole book (Evergreen Life) after having a vision of handing a pine cone to my wife! I had no idea what it meant at first, but God made it clear as I prayed and sought it out.

The simplest of words are full of power when they come from heaven. I had a vision of the younger sister of a guy at the recovery house and I described her to him. I said, "You miss her, don't you? I see God bringing you back together with your family." He replied, "That's what I've been praying for." I prayed for the owner of the pizza place. All I got was, "You're a blessing because of the jobs you give to people. Keep being a blessing." The word is simple, but it carries power when it comes from heaven.

You may see or imagine yourself giving someone money, taking them out to eat, or something else. God often speaks

## 8. God's Grace Manifests through Faith

through the imagination of a born-again heart in communion with him. Sometimes I know what I see is scriptural and in line with God's character, but I question, "Is this God, or just my imagination?" Yet I act in faith. I want people to see Jesus.

I've heard several testimonies of a Christian imagining themself paying for the groceries of the person in line in front of them and finding out that person needed help! In fact, when I was a child and my dad was unemployed, the Lord spoke to someone who left groceries on our steps without having natural knowledge of our situation. Such testimonies glorify Jesus and demonstrate God's love to people. Don't let anybody rob you spiritually by telling you to never pay attention to your heart!

## *Healing and Deliverance*

Healing and deliverance often go together. Evil spirits are involved in physical conditions more often than I would have imagined.

When someone needs healing, I first ask them to evaluate the problem. Are they feeling pain now? Do they feel pain only when they walk or move in a certain way? Is mobility limited? If they have a tumor or cyst, can they feel it externally?

Many Christians pray long prayers, saying, "God, we know you can heal…" as if they were trying to convince themselves! I encourage people to pray in a different way if they want different results. As ambassadors of Christ,[530] we focus on speaking to the condition and thanking God. "Pain, go! Be healed in Jesus' name! Thank you, Jesus!"

Although there are different ways of ministering, the heart reality matters more than the methods or words. I often hold my hand about 5 inches from the person. Something like heat, a force field, or electricity is usually tangible. I ask the person what they are feeling and I often have other people (both Christians and non-Christians) put their hands near without touching the person to feel God's power around them. Then I thank Jesus for what he's doing.

I pray briefly, pause for a few moments as God's power is sinking in, and then ask them what they feel. Once in a while the pain may increase or move. If that happens, it's a spirit so I command it to get out. However, that happens less often than it used to; I think that's because my expectation has grown so much that the evil spirit usually gives up and leaves the first time that I rebuke it.

People often feel heat or movement in their body. We want to know what they felt so that we can thank God. As we thank God for what he's doing, the manifestation increases.

People often go from being in severe pain to pain-free the first time we minister. However, if the pain reduces, mobility increases, or the tumor shrinks, I continue praying and evaluate it again. Occasionally, I've prayed several times and have to move on but the person is still feeling some symptoms. I thank God for his power remaining on the person. I encourage them with testimonies of people we prayed for repeatedly and people who God's power continued to rest on after the initial ministry until they were completely healed.

I asked everyone if I could pray for them at a church in Brasilia. A teenage girl said, "Yes." However, she didn't have any specific request. I felt inspired to step out in faith, so I asked, "How about praying for you to see without your glasses. Would you like that?" She responded, "Yes!"

I felt that the Lord led me to first rebuke any spirit affecting her vision. "In Jesus' name, every spirit affecting her vision, get out! Eyes be restored! Everything, move in place! See perfectly, 20/20 vision, in Jesus' name!"

She felt movement inside her eyes and her vision improved. God's power manifested as heat over her eyes. We prayed more and soaked her eyes with God's glory until she said she saw clearly. Then she told us, "I want to be an airplane pilot, and I needed this! I need perfect vision!"

In the previous 17 years of ministering healing, I had only seen a handful of people who wore glasses experience improvement in vision. But in that moment when the girl was healed, I decided, "I'm going to take possession of this territory

## 8. God's Grace Manifests through Faith

in the Lord!" I raised my voice, "Jesus is healing people who wear glasses! Who wants to see clearly without your glasses?" I looked for everyone I could find who was wearing glasses and prayed for them in the same way. Most felt movement in their eyes, heat, and improvement, and we prayed two or three times again. Several testified at the end that they now saw perfectly without glasses. One of our missionary girls noticed no improvement at all in her eyes, but she happened to have a sinus infection and she felt heat go through her sinuses and destroy the infection as we prayed for her eyes.

Since then, I have prayed for dozens of people in the same way. They have felt heat and movement in their eyes, then demonstrated improved or perfect vision after prayer. One received perfect vision instantly when I prayed a general prayer over all the people who had glasses. All of the others initially received improvement, then we prayed at least two or three more times, soaking them with God's glory and letting the heat over their eyes seep in, and their vision improved more as we prayed again.

I've recorded several of these testimonies on video. Many were either unable to read the Bible, or unable to read a sign in the distance without their glasses. After prayer, they read what they were previously unable to read. A stranger sat on the bench beside me as I watched my daughter play in the park. I asked if she'd like to see without glasses. She could neither read her cell phone nor read a sign in the distance without glasses. After prayer, she did both. This has become part of my new normal in Christ.

I begin praying for people's vision like this: "Thank you God, for your glory on her eyes right now. In Jesus' name, every spirit affecting her vision, get out!" I always rebuke any spirit that is affecting the vision before going on to command the eyes to be healed and see clearly. This is often effective when praying for people's vision. You may also feel that the Lord is leading you to rebuke a spirit of pain or sickness when you pray for a specific person or condition.

I've often seen deliverance happen just by praying for God's presence to manifest on a person. I pray for God's glory to manifest around them and I have them hold up their hands to feel the weight of God's glory on their hands. Then, I ask what they feel. God's glory uncovers the affliction and drives it out. Sometimes, it's as simple as the person getting dizzy and I rebuke it, the dizziness passes, and they feel light. They may also start belching or present other manifestations.

Deliverance also often happens by revelation. I see God's power on a certain part of a person's body or I see darkness there, so I hone in on that. I don't know how to explain it except that I am looking at them with God's love and I see past the natural. It's often a dark area on part of their brain. Sometimes it is a physical injury, but more often it's a spirit affecting their thinking.

When ministering healing and deliverance, keep the focus on Jesus. Refuse to be impressed with anything but him. Remember that authority comes from being sent by Jesus and identifying with Jesus. It doesn't come from your effort, your natural ability, or the volume of your voice. Clothe yourself with Christ.[531]

Mark Hemans said, "Demons are not cast out in the flesh, but in the Spirit." Sometimes Christians try to cast out demons as if it were by their natural ability. More than once, I've seen half a dozen Christians striving to get someone healed or cast out a demon, and making no progress. When they finally gave up and backed away, one person who was walking in God's glory ministered and the person was healed or the demon cast out easily.

Demons may leave with or without great manifestation. They may sometimes shake, cry, scream, run away, or throw the person on the ground. One of the most common mistakes when a demon is being dramatic is for everyone to crowd around the person shouting at the demon. Have one person minister, or at least one person at a time.

I sometimes say, "You're trying too hard!" when a person prays for healing. Trying in our own strength doesn't get any results. Yielding to the Holy Spirit does. Stop trying and yield yourself completely to the Holy Spirit. Throw yourself in

## 8. God's Grace Manifests through Faith

God's river and let it carry you away. Put your heart on the altar and let God set it on fire.

Whether we sharply rebuke the demon or simply blow on the person, God's glory burning in our hearts and released through our mouths or actions expels the demon. Others may imitate what we do naturally, but to no avail, if their hearts are not burning with holy fire.

The way I pray has changed over time. Most people who minister healing effectively learned to switch from supplication (asking God) to commanding the condition with authority and thanking God. That's how I started to see people healed.

However, I've learned that crying out to Jesus can be very effective if you are doing it with the understanding of who Jesus is, that he has revealed the Father, and his will is to heal and deliver. If you beg and plead as if Jesus had never come to reveal the Father, it's ineffective. But if you cry out, "Help, Jesus!" with the confidence that he hears and delivers you, it's powerful. There is a pleading of unbelief, but there is also a pleading in faith. My prayers in tongues are often pleading in the Spirit with groans words cannot express, weeping for people.

In the last few years, I've seen an increase in power flowing through my life. More people are being healed instantly of pain, broken bones, and tumors. The way I pray has become simpler. It's often just taking a person's hand and crying out, "Jesus! Jesus!" as if I'm saying, "Help!" And then, "Thank you Jesus!" I know I need him; I know I can do nothing by myself; and I know he answers my cry. The person is healed.

## *Power Phrases and Power Actions*

Power is released through a strong heart-mouth connection when words in agreement with God flow from hearts in communion with God. Power is also released when an action in agreement with God flows out of a heart in communion with God.

Jesus did what he saw the Father doing.[532] Once, he mixed mud with spit and put it on a guy's eyes![533] He must have seen the Father doing that.

With your spiritual ears and eyes, you may hear God say something or see him do something for a particular situation. I've also heard phrases and seen visions from heaven that have become heart-revelations of truth that applies to many situations. These phrases and actions trigger my heart, quickly taking it to a place of burning fervency.

One of those actions is standing back from a person, but just close enough to hold their hand. I bow my head before the Lord. I stand far away so that people understand Jesus is the one healing them. I am only agreeing with Jesus, and other than that, I don't want to get in the way. I bow my head to yield myself to the Holy Spirit, expecting him to heal the person, because I know that he wants to. I may say nothing at all, or just whisper, "Thank you Jesus!"

Similarly, I may have someone else pray while I stand back and say, "It's about the name of Jesus, not about who prays." I stand away as if to say, "It's not me. I'm just letting Jesus do what he wants to do." I feel it's right to pray like that at certain times, especially when people are prone to focus on me instead of on Jesus. If people are saying, "God uses Jonathan; he has a spiritual gift!" it's better for me to just get out of the way and let people know that Jesus is doing the work.

Sometimes I aggressively bless the person and yell, "Everything hurting them get out now in Jesus' name!" Yet it's not the volume, but the connection between my mouth and God's presence in my heart, that releases God's power.

The Holy Spirit told me, "Honor Jesus by honoring the members of his body." We are the body of Christ, and the revelation is that when I have everybody minister to each other, I am honoring Jesus. So, when I'm with other Christians, I get everyone to minister to each other as much as possible. I don't pray for everyone myself! This glorifies Jesus and helps people

## 8. God's Grace Manifests through Faith

to see that it's about Jesus, not about some spiritual gift and not about me. If people just see me, the results are not the same.

I also regularly have people cup their hands and pray for them to feel God's glory in their hands, or I hold my hand about five inches away from their body. The person receiving ministry usually feels heat, pressure, or a hand on their body. I often have everybody around place their hand near that area without touching the person, and it feels like sticking their hands into a force field or heat. This combines healing with a sign to demonstrate the power in the name of Jesus so that people are in awe of him.

God often heals a person when I pause and wait for a few moments. I pray a quick and simple prayer and then wait quietly for God to work as I hold the person's hand. It's a position of faith. I see God's power going into the person, then I have them test the condition.

For me, these are actions or positions that flow from a heart revelation. When I take someone's hand like that, the expectation is so strong that sometimes I'm on the brink of tears. It's like a trigger that reminds me of what Jesus has done before and causes my heart to get carried away in God's river. Not everyone ministers in the same way. What's important is not the outward method, but that what we do flows from communion with God.

Certain phrases and words flow from revelation and set my heart on fire. Here are a few of those power phrases:

**"Jesus is visiting your house today!"** Jesus said to those he sent, "If they receive you, they receive me."[534] If I go anywhere and Jesus sent me, Jesus is visiting that place.

**"Holy Spirit, glorify the name of Jesus!"** I feel like a bomb goes off when I say this. What we want with every miracle and sign is that people would see Jesus through it and his name would be honored.

**"Jesus paid the highest price for Sally's healing and full redemption. Holy Spirit, thank you for giving Jesus what**

**he deserves right now! Thank you for bringing Jesus all that he paid for!"** I was talking to a guy in a recovery house who kept saying, "I've fallen so many times. I don't deserve for God to keep working in my life." I received revelation from heaven and responded, "It's not about what you deserve. It's about what Jesus deserves! Jesus paid the highest price to redeem you, and Jesus deserves what he paid for! The Holy Spirit isn't about to give up on bringing to Jesus that which Jesus has purchased with his blood!"

**"Jesus! Thank you, Jesus!"** The name of Jesus means so much to me because I've seen his wonderful works! I've called on the name of Jesus many times and he has delivered me!

**"God, thank you that you did not withhold your only Son, but gave him up for us all, and so with him you will give us all things!**[535] **Thank you that you've given us everything in Jesus! Let your river flow here now!"** This takes off all the limits!

**May great joy come to this house in Jesus' name! May great joy come to this city, so that everybody would see Jesus and his name would be honored here!** Acts 8:8 says that great joy was in the city as Philip preached Jesus in Samaria and many were healed and delivered. This scripture passage always sets my heart on fire.

## *Works of Power, Signs, and Angelic Manifestations*

Many signs and wonders happen in God's river as the manifestation of God's love and generosity. They may happen during praise and worship, or when we are praying for people and talking about Jesus. In my experience, this also seems to be when most angelic manifestations happen.

When we lived in Rio de Janeiro, a couple came for prayer and the young woman felt God's fire on her hands as heat. The

## 8. God's Grace Manifests through Faith

next day she was wondering, "Was that real?" She looked at her hands and her ring, which had been almost white, was now scorched black!

In the beginning of this year, I overheard that a young boy, about nine years old, had a cold. I said, "Let me pray for you," and grabbed his hand. "Jesus, thank you for your fire driving out every infection!" I held his hand for a moment. He suddenly withdrew it and said, "Ouch! That's hot! It hurts!" He shook his hand as if to say, "What did you just do to me?"

Everyone laughed. I said "Breathe deep. How's your throat now? How is your breathing?" He said he didn't feel anything anymore. That sign got people's attention and demonstrated the power in Jesus' name to the people in the group so that they would honor the Lord and put their hope and expectation in him.

All kinds of other signs and wonders may be triggered by praise and the message about Jesus. They cause people to honor and worship Jesus and they confirm the gospel message. Sometimes they point to a certain passage of scripture, as the supernatural rain inside my house did.

Supernatural signs and works of power also happen as the result of obeying God in a specific situation. Mel Tari's account of the revival in Indonesia includes many of these, such as walking across rivers.[536] I met a missionary who God sent to Asia. He didn't have a ticket or money, but God said to go to the airport. He asked the Lord again what to do, and heard, "Go in the bathroom." He came out of the bathroom in the airport of another country, translated like Elijah[537] and Philip[538] were in the Bible!

Some wonders happen as we obey the Lord and he protects us. Mel Tari tells how their mission group was poisoned, but it had no effect. Those who poisoned them converted.[539] Paul shook off a viper and those on the island received Christ.[540] Brother Andrew took Bibles into the Soviet Union and God blinded the eyes of the border guards so they couldn't see the Bibles stacked up in open view.[541] God sent me to Russia, and we had a metro token fall out of thin air so we wouldn't arrive too late to an apartment where I was going to preach!

Some miraculous deliverances and signs are in response to specific prayer, such as an angel leading Christians out of prison.[542] God's power is released into these situations in the same basic way as it is for healing or deliverance.

We may also develop faith for specific signs. I often pray for people until they feel God's glory in a tangible way such as fire, weight, or electricity. I pray for Christians and non-Christians in this way. Often, I use this sign to explain the gospel, that we have access to God through Jesus.

## *Greater Works*

Jesus said that those who believed in him would do even greater works! I don't know fully what "greater works" means. I'm not sure if it means "more miraculous," because from God's perspective, everything is easy! I think "greater works" may refer to works that bring an even greater manifestation of God's love and kingdom on the earth.

Loren Cunningham received a vision that led to the founding of YWAM. (Youth With a Mission) The story is full of situational miracles, and they happened in the same way as healing and other manifestations of the Holy Spirit occur. Loren saw what God was doing, and did it. He heard what God was saying, and said it. He added his "Amen" to God's "Yes." The incredible story is related in the book "Is that Really You, God?"[543]

To me, that was a greater work! Greater faith was needed for the vision of YWAM to be fulfilled than for many healing miracles! Not because it is a big organization, but because nations and people groups were reached by God's ability.

My friend Reinhard is working towards opening 100 homes for children in Brazil. He has already opened several.[544] I also see that as a greater work because it is confronting a tremendous problem by God's ability, and not by mere human power. Reinhard lost everything when he first started, and he started again! A work like that takes perseverance.

## 8. God's Grace Manifests through Faith

I also think of David Wilkerson starting Teen Challenge, and of the people running local recovery homes in my state. That kind of work takes so much faith and perseverance! When these are done by God's power, I think of them as greater works.

I started ministering healing out of a general heart revelation from scripture of Christ's compassion for the sick. I only started giving specific words of knowledge for healing a few years later. Whether we have a specific word from God or simply feel Christ's compassion, God's invisible nature is manifest in power when we act on that heavenly reality in our heart.

Reinhard never heard a specific word from God about opening orphanages. He simply felt God's compassion for orphans as he read the Bible and communed with the Lord, so he decided to act and believe God for 100 children's homes. But Loren Cunningham had an open vision that led to YWAM.

Jesus saw Satan fall from heaven when his disciples obeyed the command to preach the gospel, cast out demons, and heal the sick.[545] Regional breakthrough comes from faithfulness in ministering on the individual level. Healing the sick and casting out demons are the easy part. Learning to pray the prayer of faith for the sick is training for those who would pray to see wars and famines end.

Who will weep for the millions suffering under the brutal regime of North Korea, and the many facing starvation in North and South Sudan? Who will weep for the orphans whose life expectancy is only about 30 years, or the victims of human trafficking? How will we pray the prayer of faith for those situations if we haven't learned to pray the prayer of faith for our own neighbors to receive healing and deliverance?

The change needed will never come by our mere human effort. Where's the love of those who are satisfied with religion that's doable without the Holy Spirit's empowerment? Where is the love of pastors who are happy with spectator Christianity in which the people depend on them?

Talk about revival and nations changing is empty if we claim to be making disciples but are not teaching every

Christian to preach the gospel, heal the sick, and cast out demons on an individual level. When local pastors talk about taking our city for God, I want to know how many of their neighbors have been healed or received deliverance.

In this chapter, we've briefly reviewed every one of the "spiritual gifts" which are more accurately called "grace effects." Every one of these manifestations of God's grace works essentially in the same way, with the same mechanics. People on earth add their "Amen" to God's "Yes," heaven's lightning flashes, and God's invisible nature manifests on this earth.

# 9. God's Lightnings Flashing Through You

## *There is So Much More*

All the books in the world couldn't contain the mighty works of Jesus![546] I've only shared a small part of what I've seen Jesus do as I've written this book. Yet I feel that I am not even living in 1% of all that is available in Christ! What I've shared with you here is just a drop in the ocean!

I have so much to grow in faith, in love, and in the knowledge of Jesus! So please let Jesus himself be your standard and learn from various people in the body of Christ. I'm just sharing the part I have to offer.

I recently had a glorious time going from house to house on a Saturday. Everybody who received prayer was healed to the best of our ability to verify at that moment. I took the hand of a lady with fibromyalgia and said, "Thank you Jesus," and the pain was gone. I prayed for a bedridden man who was feeling strong pain and undergoing cancer treatments. He felt heat on his body, started sobbing, all the pain left, and he got up and walked around normally. And more! I was again overwhelmed with God's goodness.

As I basked in the glory of what Jesus had done, I thought of the thousands of other households in my city and state that Jesus wants to visit. Although what I regularly experience seems extraordinary and extravagant to most other Christians here, what God wants to do just in my city is at least 10,000 times what I am experiencing. For God's purposes to be fulfilled in my city, thousands of other Christians must begin to walk in God's power!

## *Look for People who Want Jesus*

Living a life like this changes your perspective and your values. You get bored in church if you don't see God's grace manifesting in power. Mere human wisdom and ability may have impressed you before, but now they seem so empty. In many regions, most of the religious system values orations and fine speech as the Greeks did,[547] not the power of the gospel.

Whereas you used to hope God would send revival, now you realize that God is longing to distribute his heavenly riches, but churches don't have revival because they don't want it. They want to keep control. Many pastors think, "This is my church and these are my sheep." But they are living in rebellion against Jesus who bought the church with his blood!

Sometimes Americans come to Brazil and think a church is on-fire because of the emotion or because of the numbers. Yet in many cases, they would be shocked at what goes on inside!

Once you've seen God's power and felt his love flowing through you, your perspective changes. You see many leaders calling themselves apostles, yet preaching themselves and not Jesus. As Jesus said, they refuse to enter the Kingdom of heaven and they hinder those who want to enter.[548]

When God moves, they become jealous instead of jumping in the river. Some will tell you that you need their approval to obey Jesus by healing the sick and casting out demons!

If they would preach Christ, Christ's Spirit would be manifest. If it's not, they are preaching another Christ. If they would preach the gospel, God's power would be manifest. If it's not, they're preaching another gospel.[549]

Choose to obey God, not men![550] Once I wanted to pray for an old lady who was limping. It wasn't even in a church service but the religious leader didn't want me to pray. I didn't

## 9. God's Lightnings Flashing Through You!

ask his permission to pray for the next person! I went back to the dorm and spent three hours on the phone calling people to pray for them. One miracle after another happened over the phone. The religious establishment rejected Jesus, so I looked for those who would receive him.

Other Christians often see the miracles happening outside of church and recognize them as God's work through my life. Many say, "Jonathan has a spiritual gift." Yet in my experience, most of these church people fail to understand that the results in my life are different because I believe differently. They show little interest in learning from an ordinary Christian who weeps for people and has a life full of miracles, deliverance, and wonders. But they keep listening to religious leaders who lack power. They allow a church system that consumes their energy and resources to keep them from obeying Jesus. They pay attention to those who slap them around and abuse them,[551] but overlook those who come to serve them! Their leaders often receive those who dishonor Jesus, yet dishonor those who preach Jesus.

Their churches don't have revival because it isn't what they value. They don't have the Spirit of Christ manifest among them in power because that's not what is important to them. The apostle Paul said, "Everyone is seeking their own interests, and not those of Christ Jesus."[552] Unfortunately, this is frequently true today. Leaders want the people's tithes, and the people boast in their tithes, but they don't care at all for the orphans, homeless, and oppressed all around them. There seem to be few exceptions to this, and they are precious!

Jesus said the kingdom of heaven is like a king who prepared a wedding banquet for his son. His servants sought those who had been invited, but the invited guests refused to come. They paid no attention and went off to their fields and businesses. Some even mistreated and killed his messengers. The king sent his army against them. Then he told his servants to go out on the street corners and invite anyone they could find until the wedding hall was filled with guests.[553]

If Jesus has sent you, then he who receives you receives Jesus, and he who rejects you rejects Jesus.[554] Jesus came humble and riding on a donkey,[555] and his ambassadors come in the same way. It takes humility to receive them.

Jesus said that if you go and they don't receive you, shake the dust off your feet and go to the next town.[556] Look for those who are hungry. Jesus said, "Blessed are the poor in spirit, for theirs is the kingdom of heaven."[557] Find people who are messed up, who have problems, and preach Jesus to them! They are often the ones who receive. If you want to witness God's manifest power and glory, show God's love to people whom others consider hopeless. And believe for them!

In making a list of my recorded testimonies, I discovered hundreds. Yet the testimonies I've written here and in other books, blog posts, and journals are just the highlights, from 1-10% of everything I've seen Jesus do. I've seen Jesus heal thousands of people, working not as a full-time minister but as a construction worker and an English teacher.

I cry aloud to Jesus when I face people's needs, knowing I need the Holy Spirit's help and can do nothing without him! To know our need for God is to be poor in spirit. Yet many Christians think they are rich and act as if they don't need God's power! If they truly loved the broken, in action and in truth,[558] they would know how much they need the Holy Spirit!

If you don't weep with Jesus, you don't know very well who he is! We enter into fellowship with Jesus by making his priorities our priorities and by going out to rescue those whom he is rescuing.

Look for healthy fellowship with other Christians in meetings that are done decently and in order. The Biblical idea of a meeting done decently and in order is a meeting in which the various members of the body of Christ minister with God's supernatural grace.[559] It's not a one-man show keeping people in passive dependence on the person in front. Rather, if a prophet speaks and a revelation comes to someone who is seated, the first prophet should stop to allow the other one to speak![560]

9. God's Lightnings Flashing Through You!

You may find such fellowship in a men's or ladies' group, Bible study, or prayer group. If you can't find such a meeting, consider hosting one!

## *Knowing Jesus and Making Him Known*

I love the YWAM vision: to know Jesus and make him known. That is what motivates me. You can get so used to the supernatural that the thrill doesn't keep you going anymore. It takes perseverance to keep walking in God's power. What keeps me going is that I see Jesus with the eyes of my heart when he touches people. I want other people to see Jesus and to experience his glory as I have. That creates fervency in my prayers.

May that be what drives you. If our motivation is getting more people to come to our church, raising our status, or anything else, it is easy to burn out. As we walk in the supernatural, we realize how overwhelming the need is and how helpless we are without the Holy Spirit. But love keeps us going. We all need to ask God to baptize us in his love.

May our lives be consumed with Jesus Christ. Then, we will have given our lives for something eternal.

I teach English six days a week and have a wife and two kids. This life of miracles is for every disciple of Jesus, not only those who are in full-time ministry!

Don't be satisfied with where you are. I'm not! I'm so thankful for all God has done, but I need to walk in more! It's amazing how many people who don't walk in God's power will not admit that they need to confront their own unbelief. Yet I've had the supernatural experiences I share in this book and many more, and I've often recognized and confronted my own unbelief.

Pray, "God, open the eyes of my heart to see Jesus!" Cry out for wisdom and correction![561] Act in aggressive faith. Refuse to be satisfied with anything less than revival now! Persevere! You'll see God do far more than you could have ever asked or imagined by his power at work in you![562]

# About The Author

Jonathan Brenneman was born in Rochester, New York and raised in Pennsylvania. Although a troubled child, he was at the same time very religious. He read the Bible from cover to cover when he was seven years old, all the while questioning and wondering about the existence of God.

When Jonathan was nine years old, he woke up one morning with bad back pain. His mother prayed for him. To his surprise, he felt something like a hot ball of energy rolling up and down inside his back. The pain melted away. He later told his friends, "I know that God is real. I felt his hand on my back."

In spite of this experience, Jonathan still had no peace. He prayed the "sinner's prayer" but with no change until two years later when he had a born-again experience. It felt like heaven opened and unexplainable joy and peace descended upon him! He was different, and knew it! The things he'd felt so guilty about and tried unsuccessfully to change, were simply gone.

Jonathan dedicated his life to the Lord as a missionary, going on his first mission trip at age fourteen. As a teenager and young adult, he continued to travel and learn languages. During a time of desperation when he was twenty-one, God touched him powerfully at a Christian conference. It was the beginning of growing in a supernatural lifestyle. Many amazing miracles and healings began to happen.

In between construction jobs, Jonathan began visiting churches in the United States, Canada, Latin America, and Eastern Europe. He has preached in four languages and his ministry journeys have included Russia, Ukraine, Poland, Italy, Canada, Mexico, Belize, and Brazil. In these places, Jonathan has taught and encouraged believers, shared Christ with unbelievers, and prayed for thousands of people. He's often worked with children and seniors. Jonathan considers it a tremendous privilege to serve the people Jesus gave his life for.

In spite of great difficulty, Jonathan moved to Brazil in 2012. He spent seven years in Rio de Janeiro and is now a missionary in Goiânia with his wife Elizabeth and two daughters. He is involved in evangelistic outreaches, supporting local rescue missions, caring for the poor, and teaching the church to do the works Jesus did.

# Heaven Now Missions

As of this book's publication in 2024, Jonathan works six days a week teaching English. He goes on missions on his day off, on some weeknights, and occasionally during the day between classes. He often takes hours off or uses vacation days for missions such as the recent trip to Marajó Island.

Marajó is an island the size of Switzerland at the mouth of the Amazon River, and has thousands of villages with no gospel presence. Child prostitution and incest are rampant. Jonathan traveled 20 hours by boat to a region where most people had never seen a doctor in their lives. He wants to return.

Jonathan's desire is to train others, care for the poor, and reach those who have never heard the gospel. He is heavily involved in local rescue missions and evangelistic outreaches. Donations to Heaven Now Missions go first towards mercy ministries such as helping rescue missions with food, soap, and geriatric diapers. They also cover mission expenses and the purchase of Bibles for distribution. Currently, a small percentage of donations also goes towards missionary support. This helps to pay the bills when so much time is given to ministry.

Tax-deductable contributions may be made through Joshua's Army. See the Heaven Now Missions page at www.gotoheavennow.com for information on making a one-time or monthly contribution.

# Contact

You can get in touch with Jonathan by emailing jonathan@gotoheavennow.com. See his blog at www.gotoheavennow.com, his Amazon author page, his Goodreads page, and his Facebook author page, Jonathan Brenneman.

See the Heaven Now Missions page for information on supporting Jonathan's work in Brazil.

Amazon reviews are the author's tip jar! They also help to get the message out to more people. If you have enjoyed this book, please consider leaving a review on Goodreads and/or Amazon.com.

# Also By Jonathan Brenneman

*I Am Persuaded: Christian Leadership as Taught by Jesus.*

*The Power and Love Sandwich: Why You Should Seek God's Face AND His Hand*

*Present Access to Heaven (#1 Heaven Now Series)*

*I Will Awaken the Dawn (#2 Heaven Now Series)*

*Jesus Has Come in the Flesh (#3 Heaven Now Series)*

*What Really Causes Needless Casualties of War?: Why We Do Have Authority Over All Satan's Power, and Why People Get Hurt*

*Evergreen Life: Flourish in Every Circumstance*

*Are You My Spiritual Father?: Spiritual Fathers and Sons…or Brothers?*

*Refuting Fallacious Criticisms of Signs and Wonders: Escape the Deception of Attributing God's Work to the Devil*

*The Trojan Horse of Tithing: How Tithe Traditions Have Undermined a Pure Gospel Message*

# References

1. 1 John 1:5
2. 1 John 4:8
3. 1 Timothy 1:17
4. Romans 11:36
5. John 17:3
6. Romans 3:23
7. Romans 6:23
8. Proverbs 14:12
9. John 10:10
10. Colossians 1:15
11. Isaiah 59:2
12. Leviticus 16:21
13. Isaiah 53:4-5 YLT
14. Hebrews 2:14, Colossians 2:14
15. Romans 5:8
16. Acts 3:15
17. Acts 2:24
18. Mark 1:15, Acts 2:21
19. Romans 6:6, Galatians 2:20
20. Colossians 3:1, Ephesians 2:6, Colossians 2:12
21. John 16:8
22. Acts 9:35
23. Ephesians 5:8
24. Acts 2:38
25. Romans 6:3-4
26. Galatians 3:27
27. Galatians 3:16, Hebrews 1:12, 2 Corinthians 1:20
28. Galatians 3:29
29. 1 Corinthians 11:26
30. Colossians 2:6-7
31. 2 Corinthians 13:14, 2 Corinthians 6:14
32. 2 Corinthians 11:14
33. Deuteronomy 7:26, Acts 19:19
34. Hebrews 1:3

35 https://en.wikipedia.org/wiki/Jo%C3%A3o_Teixeira_de_Faria
36 Proverbs 14:12
37 http://dominionfire.com/yoga-and-mental-illness-aspen-morrow/
38 1 John 4:1
39 John 14:6, John 10:1-10
40 Hebrews 1:14
41 1 Timothy 2:5
42 Hebrews 1:2-4
43 Hebrews 1:6
44 Revelation 22:9
45 Mark 9:25
46 https://www.reddit.com/r/NoFap/comments/wwiuan/nofap/
47 Romans 6:16-23
48 Romans 14:17
49 Hebrews 10:16, Ephesians 2:8
50 Romans 5:17
51 Galatians 2:20
52 Luke 3:16
53 Mark 11:24
54 Luke 11:13
55 John 3:3-8
56 Psalm 34:8
57 Romans 10:12
58 Romans 8:32
59 Psalm 84:11
60 Exodus 15:26
61 Colossians 3:15
62 Psalm 104:4
63 Psalm 71:15, Psalm 40:5
64 John 21:25
65 Luke 1:37
66 Ephesians 3:20
67 Mark 9:23
68 Psalm 62:11-12, Psalm 63:2, 1 Peter 4:11, Psalm 29:1, Romans 1:20
69 John 2:11
70 1 John 3:17-18
71 James 2:14-18, 20, 22
72 Mark 8:2-3, Matthew 9:35-36, Matthew 14:14

73 1 John 1:1-3
74 1 Corinthians 4:20
75 John 14:9
76 Matthew 14:14, Matthew 20:34, Luke 7:13, Matthew 15:42
77 Hebrews 13:8
78 Lamentations 3:22-23
79 John 1:1, 14
80 Hebrews 4:12
81 2 Corinthians 3:6
82 John 5:39-40
83 1 John 4:2
84 Luke 4:14
85 Colossians 1:15, John 14:9, Hebrews 1:3
86 John 1:14
87 Romans 5:17, 2 Peter 1:2
88 1 Timothy 3:16
89 1 Corinthians 12:27, Colossians 1:18, 24, Ephesians 1:22-23
90 1 Corinthians 6:19
91 https://gotoheavennow.com/the-misconception-of-spiritual-gifts-part-1-grace-effects-rather-than-spiritual-gifts/
92 Matthew 10:7
93 1 Corinthians 4:20
94 Luke 9:1, Matthew 10:1
95 Matthew 10:7-8
96 Matthew 28:19-20
97 John 20:21
98 Acts 1:4
99 John 20:21
100 John 14:12
101 Mark 16:17-18
102 John 17:22
103 John 14:21, 23-24 NKJV
104 2 Corinthians 3:13, 2 Corinthians 4:6, Acts 6:15
105 Acts 4:13
106 1 Corinthians 2:4
107 John 5:19
108 Luke 13:16
109 John 1:14

110 Matthew 20:30-31, Mark 10:47, Luke 17:13
111 John 18:6, Mark 9:20, Acts 26:14, Revelation 1:17
112 Matthew 11:5
113 Mark 7:31-37
114 Mark 3:11, Luke 4:41
115 Revelation 3:17
116 1 Corinthians 3:12-13
117 Luke 12:21
118 2 Corinthians 11:4
119 Strong's Greek: 4102. πίστις (pistis) -- faith, faithfulness
120 John 14:9
121 Hebrews 1:2
122 2 Timothy 2:2
123 James 5:14
124 Hebrews 13:8-9
125 1 Corinthians 11:1
126 Romans 15:18-19
127 2 Corinthians 2:1-4
128 2 Corinthians 3:6
129 1 Corinthians 4:20
130 Titus 1:9, 2 Thessalonians 2:15
131 Mark 1:22, Matthew 7:29
132 1 Corinthians 3:19
133 1 Peter 5:3
134 Luke 24:46-49
135 James 4:6, 1 Peter 5:5
136 2 Timothy 3:7
137 Galatians 3:1-9
138 2 Timothy 3:5
139 Mark 8:15, Matthew 16:6
140 Galatians 5:1-9
141 Matthew 5:13
142 Tari, Mel. Like A Mighty Wind Page 63-65
143 Romans 10:9
144 Matthew 23:15
145 Matthew 28:19
146 Jeremiah 33:3
147 2nd Corinthians 3:5-6

148 Luke 10:21, Matthew 11:25
149 Romans 1:16
150 Matthew 9:36, Matthew 14:14
151 2 Corinthians 4:6
152 2 Peter 3:18, Colossians 1:10
153 2 Peter 1:4
154 Mark 4:9, Matthew 11:5, Matthew 13:9
155 http://gotoheavennow.com/the-misconception-of-spiritual-gifts-part-1-grace-effects-rather-than-spiritual-gifts/
156 Matthew 11:25
157 https://www.wiebefamily.org/spiritual_gifts.htm Charismata. "Charis" meaning "grace" and the suffix "mata" meaning "effects/results."
158 http://www.christinyou.net/pages/chrsmata.html
159 http://gotoheavennow.com/?s=Spiritual+gifts
160 John 7:38
161 http://gotoheavennow.com/the-spiritual-gifts-are-for-all-christians/
162 Mark Hemans message. It is Jesus. Online: https://www.youtube.com/watch?v=mJHOaAhzlTc 1:33:22-1:35:10
163 Luke 22:42
164 Colossians 2:9-10
165 Ephesians 3:20
166 Colossians 1:10, 2 Peter 3:18
167 Acts 13:52, 1 Corinthians 12:13, Acts 11:24, Ephesians 5:18-19
168 1 Corinthians 2:12
169 2 Corinthians 5:20
170 2 Corinthians 1:20
171 John 5:30
172 Luke 10:2
173 John 6:35
174 Ephesians 1:3
175 Acts 10:34
176 Romans 10:12
177 Ephesians 3:20
178 Luke 1:37, Matthew 19:26
179 Mark 9:23
180 1 Timothy 3:16
178 1 John 4:2-3
182 John 14:12

183 Genesis 1:25
184 Genesis 1:31
185 Genesis 2:8
186 Genesis 1:26-28, 2:15
187 Psalm 115:16
188 John 4:24
189 Colossians 1:15, Hebrews 11:27, John 1:18, 1 Timothy 6:16, 1 Timothy 1:17
190 Genesis 1:26
191 Hebrews 2:5-8
192 Hebrews 2:8 The Common English Bible (CEB), The Easy to Read Version (ERV), The Expanded Bible (EXB), God's Word Translation (GW), International Children's Bible (ICB), J.B. Phillips New Testament (PHILLIPS), Names of God Bible (NOG), New Century Version (NCV), New English Translation (NET), New International Reader's Version (NIRV), and the Amplified Bible (AMP) are some of the versions that render "put all things under his feet) as "put everything under their control."
193 See my book "Jesus Has Come in the Flesh" for more detailed explanation of this.
194 Romans 3:23, Isaiah 59:1-15
195 Isaiah 59:16
196 Psalm 33:11
197 Job 9:32
198 John 1:18
199 Colossians 1:15
200 John 14:9
201 Isaiah 7:14, Matthew 1:23
202 Romans 5:12-17
203 John 17:3
204 2 Corinthians 4:18
205 Hebrews 11:3
206 2 Corinthians 1:20
207 Matthew 6:10
208 Hebrews 11:1, Hebrews 11:27
209 Ephesians 1:9
210 Matthew 14:14
211 Exodus 15:26
212 Psalms 33:10-11
213 1 Corinthians 15:57, 2 Corinthians 2:14
214 Deuteronomy 10:18, Psalms 68:5, Psalms 82:3, Psalms 146:7-9
215 Isaiah 53:4-5 YLT

216 2 Corinthians 1:20
217 Hebrews 1:2
218 Genesis 3:1
219 2 Corinthians 4:6
220 Matthew 14:36, Mark 6:56, Luke 6:19, Matthew 15:29-31, Matthew 8:16
221 Ephesians 1:18
222 Ephesians 1:22-23, Colossians 1:24, Ephesians 5:23, 1 Corinthians 12:27
223 2 Corinthians 11:14
224 John 14:6
225 1 Corinthians 12:3
226 2 Corinthians 3:18
227 2 Corinthians 4:18
228 John 5:39
229 Luke 24:32
230 Psalm 115:4-8, Psalm 135:15-18
231 2 Corinthians 4:6
232 2 Corinthians 3:18
233 Matthew 15:6, Mark 7:13
234 Matthew 14:14
235 Colossians 1:9-12
236 Hebrews 11:6
237 Hebrews 2:17
238 Hebrews 4:15
239 Mark 11:12, Matthew 4:2
240 2 Corinthians 13:4, Matthew 26:41
241 John 4:6
242 1 Peter 3:18
243 Matthew 4:11, Luke 22:43
244 Luke 8:3, Mark 15:41
245 John 5:19
246 1 Corinthians 11:1, Ephesians 5:1
247 Matthew 4:19
248 John 14:12
249 John 5:30
250 See my book "Jesus has Come in the Flesh" for more detail.
251 Matthew 10:8
252 Colossians 2:19
253 https://www.explainthatstuff.com/capacitors.html

254 (https://science.howstuffworks.com/nature/natural-disasters/lightning4.htm)

255 1 Corinthians 6:17

256 Ephesians 3:16

257 Colossians 1:29

258 Healed from Cancer and Mad at God. Online: https://www.youtube.com/watch?v=s0ntsTxwnrw

259 Matthew 17:20

260 Bonnke, Reinhard. Even Greater. Orlanda, USA. Full Flame LLC, 2004. Page 139.

261 Matthew 17:20

262 Matthew 14:36, Luke 6:19, Mark 6:56

263 Psalm 97:5

264 Psalm 66:10, Zechariah 13:9, Malachi 3:3

265 2 Corinthians 4:18

266 2 Corinthians 6:2

267 2 Kings 13:14-19

268 2 Corinthians 4:18

269 Psalm 107:20

270 Ephesians 6:17

271 Matthew 13:3-8

272 Hebrews 2:4

273 Ephesians 6:17

274 Psalm 149:6

275 Ezekiel 47

276 1 Corinthians 3:16

277 John 7:38

278 Hebrews 9:24

279 Hebrews 10:19-22

280 Hebrews 2:11

281 Isaiah 64:1

282 1 Thessalonians 5:17

283 Isaiah 65:24

284 Romans 1:16

285 Ephesians 1:20-23, 2:6

286 Matthew 1:23

287 John 10:9

288 John 14:6

289 2 Corinthians 1:20

290 Ephesians 2:8

291 Colossians 2:6
292 Galatians 2:21, Galatians 5:4
293 Exodus 23:15
294 Galatians 4:21-31
295 Isaiah 55:1
296 1 Peter 5:5, James 4:6
297 Luke 1:53
298 2 Corinthians 11:3
299 Colossians 2:6
300 Isaiah 53:5
301 Shalom Strong's Hebrew word 7965
302 Sozo Strong's Greek word 4982
303 1 Corinthians 1:20
304 1 Corinthians 8:7-9, Romans 5:17
305 Luke 4:18
306 Ephesians 1:3, 2 Peter 1:3
307 Colossians 2:10
308 Ephesians 1:3
309 2nd Peter 1:3
310 Romans 4:14, Galatians 3:9-10, 3:18, 5:4
311 Galatians 3:1-5
312 Matthew 16:11-12
313 1 Corinthians 5:7-8
314 Galatians 5:9
315 Galatians 1:6-7
316 Acts 3:12
317 John 12:24
318 Matthew 23:11
319 Matthew 25:40
320 Luke 1:53
321 Colossians 2:12, Romans 6:4
322 Romans 6:11
323 Romans 3:23
324 2 Corinthians 5:17
325 Colossians 3:3-12
326 1 Corinthians 1:2, Romans 1:7, Romans 16:15, Romans 8:27, Philippians 4:22, Colossians 1:26, Acts 9:32, and many others.
327 Romans 5:17

328 Romans 6:19
329 Ephesians 5:8
330 2 Corinthians 6:14
331 1 John 1:5
332 Ephesians 5:8
333 For a more detailed study of this, see my article https://gotoheavennow.com/what-does-the-flesh-mean-in-the-bible/
334 Genesis 17:11
335 Romans 8:9
336 Hebrews 4:16, Ephesians 3:12
337 Exodus 34:29-35
338 2 Corinthians 3:7-18
339 Acts 6:15
340 Hebrews 2:11
341 Hebrew 4:16
342 Hebrews 2:14
343 Colossians 2:15
344 Colossians 2:13-14
345 Romans 7:1-6
346 Romans 8:2
347 Romans 14:17
348 1 Corinthians 3:4
349 Colossians 3:2
350 Colossians 3:5
351 1 Corinthians 1:25
352 Ephesians 1:21
353 Luke 9:1, Matthew 10:1
354 Galatians 2:20
355 1 Peter 1:8-9
356 Psalm 23:1
357 Romans 8:25
358 Proverbs 28:1
359 Romans 5:8
360 1 John 4:10
361 1 John 4:19
362 James 4:6
363 Luke 10:20
364 2 Corinthians 4:5

365 Ephesians 1:3
366 Colossians 2:10
367 Paradeisos Strong's Greek word 3857
368 Genesis 2:8-15
369 Genesis 3:23-24
370 1 Corinthians 15:45
371 Ephesians 3:12
372 Hebrews 9:24
373 1 Corinthians 3:16
374 1 John 4:12, 1 John 3:24, Revelation 21:3
375 Ezekiel 48:35
376 Luke 8:11
377 Ezekiel 47:1
378 Genesis 2:10
379 Galatians 6:9
380 1 Thessalonians 5:18, Psalm 34:1
381 Colossians 3:1-3
382 Psalm 111:2
383 Psalm 77:11-12, Psalm 105:5, Psalm 78:4
384 1 John 1:7
385 Romans 13:12
386 Ephesians 5:11
387 Hebrews 2:5
388 Hebrews 4:16
389 1 Corinthians 2:9-12
390 Explanation of resonance: https://byjus.com/physics/resonance/
391 1 Corinthians 6:17
392 Psalm 42:7
393 Isaiah 30:15-17
394 Hebrews 11:6
395 2 Corinthians 3:5
396 Ephesians 6:10
397 Colossians 1:11, 2:6-7, Ephesians 3:16, 1 Peter 5:10, 2 Thessalonians 2:17, etc.
398 1 John 2:14
399 Ephesians 2:22
400 Colossians 2:8-10
401 Romans 4:20
402 Ephesians 6:14

403 James 3:4-5
404 Psalm 103:1
405 Ephesians 5:18-19
406 1 Thessalonians 5:18
407 See the following article for more detailed explanation: https://gotoheavennow.com/i-will-sing-your-praise-before-the-gods/
408 Ephesians 1:18
409 Psalm 119:32
410 Luke 1:37
411 Mark 9:23
412 Romans 8:32
413 Ephesians 4:15
414 Ephesians 3:16
415 Ephesians 3:20
416 John 14:14
417 Romans 13:14
418 1 Corinthians 6:15, 1 Corinthians 12:27
419 Ephesians 3:19
420 Colossians 1:27
421 2 Peter 1:3-4
422 2 Peter 1:2
423 Romans 8:32
424 John 17:22-23
425 Colossians 2:9
426 Colossians 2:10
427 Matthew 17:20, Mark 9:23
428 Ephesians 3:20
429 Colossians 2:20, Galatians 2:20
430 Ephesians 2:6
431 Ephesians 1:18-23
432 Luke 10:19
433 Matthew 10:1
434 Hebrews 4:16
435 https://gotoheavennow.com/present-access-to-heaven/
436 Ephesians 1:3
437 Colossians 2:3
438 1 Corinthians 1:30
439 John 10:3

440 Romans 1:16
441 Luke 6:19
442 Exodus 15:26
443 1 Corinthians 12:27
444 Romans 8:10, 2 Corinthians 13:5, Galatians 2:20, Ephesians 3:17, Colossians 1:27
445 1 Corinthians 1:30, 2 Corinthians 5:17, Galatians 3:26, Romans 8:1-2, 1 Corinthians 15:22, Romans 16:7, Ephesians 2:10, Ephesians 1:3, Ephesians 2:13, Ephesians 1:7, Galatians 3:27
446 https://gotoheavennow.com/jesus-still-comes-to-us-humble-and-riding-on-a-donkey/
447 Matthew 10:40
448 2 Corinthians 12:9
449 2 Corinthians 1:8-9
450 Matthew 14:36, Mark 6:56, Luke 6:19
451 Hebrews 2:17
452 Psalm 97:5
453 Hebrews 11:27, 2 Corinthians 4:18
454 Matthew 17:20
455 Psalm 33:6, Hebrews 11:3, Colossians 1:16, John 1:3
456 Genesis 1:27
457 Psalm 115:16
458 Romans 5:17
459 2 Corinthians 5:20
460 John 1:14
461 Romans 10:9
462 John 20:21
463 Mark 9:23
464 2 Corinthians 4:13
465 Romans 5:17
466 Proverbs 18:21
467 Matthew 12:34
468 Romans 10:9
469 2 Corinthians 4:13
470 1 Samuel 3:19
471 Psalms 12:2
472 James 1:7-8
473 2 Timothy 2:16, Job 15:3, Proverbs 14:23, etc.
474 Matthew 7:29
475 Matthew 8:16

476 1 Corinthians 15:47-49
477 Psalm 107:20
478 2 Chronicles 5:13-14
479 Psalm 22:3
480 2 Chronicles 20:1-29
481 Acts 16:22-31
482 Ephesians 5:19
483 Psalm 103:20
484 Psalm 86:11+12
485 Psalm 9:1, 86:12, 111:1, 138:1
486 Psalm 103:1
487 Ephesians 1:21, Ephesians 2:6
488 Romans 6:4
489 Hebrews 2:14
490 Psalm 23:4
491 Isaiah 8:12-13
492 1 John 4:18
493 Luke 10:19
494 Colossians 1:13
495 1 John 4:4
496 Matthew 5:44
497 Hebrews 4:9-10
498 James 5:16
499 Psalm 119:32
500 James 3:4-5
501 Matthew 15:18
502 Proverbs 18:21
503 Romans 1:21
504 1 Thessalonians 5:18
505 Psalm 111:2
506 2 Peter 1:4
507 Hebrews 1:14
508 2 Corinthians 1:20
509 Romans 8:32
510 Ephesians 3:20
511 Isaiah 65:24
512 1 Corinthians 1:31, Jeremiah 9:24
513 Psalm 34:1-2

514 Psalm 40:5

515 John 7:38

516 Interview with Jackie Pullinger: https://www.youtube.com/watch?v=1ARw35TDAnM

517 1 Corinthians 14:4, Jude 1:20

518 Romans 8:26-27

519 1 Corinthians 14:29

520 I learned this at the Inside Out Training and Equipping School. I was a trainer with them for some time. You can find them on Facebook!

521 Jeremiah 17:9

522 Ezekiel 36:26, Jeremiah 31:31-34

523 John 15:7

524 Isaiah 55:11

525 John 2:5

526 Psalm 130:5

527 Psalm 131:2

528 Proverbs 3:5

529 James 1:5-8

530 2 Corinthians 5:20

531 Romans 13:14, Galatians 3:27

532 John 5:19

533 John 9:6

534 Matthew 10:40

535 Romans 8:32

536 Tari, Mel. Dudley, Cliff. Like a Mighty Wind. New Leaf Press. 1995. Pg. 43

537 2 Kings 2:16

538 Acts 8:39-40

539 Tari, Mel; Dudley, Cliff. Like a Mighty Wind. New Leaf Press. 1995. Pg. 40.

540 Acts 28:3-6

541 Brother Andrew; Sherill, John and Elizabeth. God's Smuggler. Chosen Books. 2015

542 Acts 12:7-11

543 Cunningham, Loren; Rogers, Janice. Is That Really You, God?: Hearing the Voice of God. YWAM Publishing. 2001

544 Online: https://braziliankidskare.org/home-nv-eg/

545 Luke 10:17-18

546 John 21:25

547 1 Corinthians 1:22

548 Matthew 23:13

549 2 Corinthians 11:4

550 Acts 5:29
551 2 Corinthians 11:20
552 Philippians 2:21
553 Matthew 22:1-14
554 Matthew 10:40
555 Matthew 21:5
556 Luke 9:5
557 Matthew 5:3
558 1 John 3:18
559 1 Corinthians 14
560 1 Corinthians 14:29-33
561 Proverbs 2:3-5
562 Ephesians 3:20

Printed in Great Britain
by Amazon